THE ULTIMAT
AIR FRYER

COOKBOOK FOR BEGINNERS

GET YOUR
BONUS
100% FREE
SCAN THE QR CODE OR GO TO
https://sites.google.com/view/freebonusbooks

You don't need to enter any details

except your e-mail

GET YOUR FREE BONUS PASSWORD ON PAGE 23

Table of Contents

INTRODUCTION

Greetings, fellow food enthusiast! Welcome to my special air fryer cookbook, where we're about to embark on an exciting culinary journey that will revolutionize your cooking experience. If, like me, you adore the irresistible crunch of fried food but also aim for a healthier approach, you're in for a delightful surprise.

Air frying is like having a kitchen wizard at your disposal. It revolves around using hot air to cook your favorite dishes to crispy perfection, without drowning them in oil.

Picture this: crispy french fries, succulent chicken tenders, or delectable snacks, all with a fraction of the calories and fat compared to traditional frying. That's the enchantment of air frying!

But here's the best part - it's not just about making your beloved fried treats healthier. Air frying is incredibly versatile. You can roast veggies, bake cookies, reheat leftovers, and more, all with this handy appliance. Plus, it's a breeze to use. Simply set the temperature and time, put in your food, and let the air fryer work its culinary magic. No more fretting over oil splatters or messy cleanups. This cookbook is brimming with the fundamentals of air frying and mouthwatering recipes for you to savor with your family.

Consider this more than just a cookbook; it's a portal to a culinary adventure that invites you to discover the magic of air frying. As we embark on this journey together, remember that my aim is straightforward: to empower you with the knowledge and inspiration to transform everyday ingredients into extraordinary creations.

CHAPTER 1

ALL YOU NEED TO KNOW ABOUT AIR FRYING

Air frying has become a popular cooking method, known for its capacity to create crispy, golden-brown foods reminiscent of deep frying, but with a notable reduction in the use of oil. The technique involves the rapid circulation of hot air around the food to ensure even cooking. Let's delve into how the air frying process unfolds:

1. **Heating Element**: Inside the air fryer, a robust heating element, usually situated at the top, generates the necessary heat for cooking.

2. **Fan System**: Positioned above the heating element, a powerful fan directs hot air downward onto the food in the cooking basket or tray.

3. **Cooking Chamber**: The cooking chamber is where the culinary magic unfolds. It's the designated space inside the air fryer where the food is carefully placed, designed to facilitate efficient airflow.

4. **Food Placement**: Arrange food items in a single layer within the cooking basket or on the cooking tray. Avoid overcrowding to ensure proper circulation of hot air.

5. **Maillard Reaction**: When the hot air meets the food's surface, it initiates the Maillard reaction. This chemical process is responsible for the appealing browning and crisping, enhancing the texture and flavor of the food.

6. **Cooking Time and Temperature**: Take command of the cooking process by adjusting time and temperature settings on the air fryer's control panel or interface. Different foods may require specific settings, which can be found in recipes or tailored to your preferences.

7. **Minimal Oil:** A key benefit of air frying is its minimal oil requirement. Unlike traditional deep frying, most air fryer recipes suggest a light coating of oil on the food's surface, often applied with a spray bottle.

8. **Health Benefits:** Air frying is often hailed as a healthier alternative to deep frying because it significantly reduces the intake of unhealthy trans fats and calories. It maintains the taste and texture of fried foods without the excess oil.

9. **Versatility:** Air fryers are adaptive kitchen tools that can cook a variety of items, including crispy appetizers, hearty dishes, and sweet desserts. You may air fry fresh ingredients, frozen foods, and even leftovers.

Setting Up Your Air Fryer

Congratulations on your new air fryer! Before you start air frying, it's essential to get acquainted with your appliance and ensure it's ready for action. This section will guide you through the initial setup process, so you can start creating delicious and healthy dishes in no time.

STEP 1: Unboxing Your Air Fryer

Begin by carefully unboxing your air fryer. Check for any visible damage or missing parts. Most air fryers typically come with the following components:

- The main cooking unit

- A removable basket or tray

- A non-stick coating or air fryer liner

- A user manual (if included)

- Accessories like racks or skewers (if applicable)

Inspect each component to make sure everything is in good condition and that no packaging materials remain inside.

STEP 2: Choosing a Suitable Location

Select a stable, flat, and heat-resistant surface for your air fryer. Ensure there's ample space around it for proper air circulation and ventilation. Keep the appliance away from flammable materials, water sources, and other heat-sensitive items.

STEP 3. Power Requirements

Verify that your air fryer is compatible with your electrical system. Most air fryers are designed for standard household outlets (120V in the United States). Check the manufacturer's instructions for specific voltage and wattage requirements.

STEP 4. Preparing Your Air Fryer Basket or Tray

Before using your air fryer for the first time, it's a good idea to wash the basket or tray, as well as any included accessories, with warm, soapy water. Rinse and dry them thoroughly to remove any manufacturing residues or dust.

STEP 5. Seasoning Your Air Fryer (If Necessary)

Some air fryers may recommend seasoning the cooking surfaces with a thin layer of cooking oil to prevent sticking. Refer to your user manual for any specific seasoning instructions. Not all models require this step.

STEP 6. Plug It In

Once your air fryer is set up in its designated location, plug it into a suitable electrical outlet. Make sure the cord is safely out of the way to avoid any tripping hazards.

With your air fryer now set up and ready to go, you're one step closer to enjoying crispy, flavorful dishes with less oil and hassle. In the following section, we'll check out the essential tools and accessories that will enhance your air frying experience.

Essential Tools and Accessories

Now that your air fryer is set up and ready to use, it's time to explore the essential tools and accessories that will elevate your air frying experience. These items will help you prepare, cook, and serve delicious meals effortlessly.

1. Cooking Oil Spray Bottle

A cooking oil spray bottle is a must-have accessory for air frying. It allows you to apply a fine mist of oil to your food, ensuring even coating without excess oil. Choose a refillable, non-aerosol spray bottle to control the type and amount of oil you use.

2. Silicone Tongs or Cooking Utensils

Silicone-tipped tongs or cooking utensils are perfect for flipping and turning food in your air fryer. They're heat-resistant and won't scratch the non-stick surface of your air fryer basket or tray.

3. Meat Thermometer

For perfectly cooked meats every time, invest in a reliable meat thermometer. It helps you monitor the internal temperature of your dishes, ensuring they reach the desired level of doneness without overcooking.

4. Parchment Paper or Liners

Parchment paper or pre-cut air fryer liners make cleanup a breeze. They prevent food from sticking to the basket or tray and reduce the need for excessive oil. Make sure to use parchment paper specifically designed for air frying.

5. Cooking Racks and Skewers

Many air fryers come with cooking racks or skewers as accessories. These allow you to cook multiple items at once or prepare kebabs and skewer-based recipes. Check if your air fryer includes these accessories or consider purchasing them separately.

6. Silicone Baking Cups

Silicone baking cups are versatile tools for making individual portions of snacks, muffins, or egg dishes in your air fryer. They're reusable and easy to clean, making them a sustainable choice.

7. Basting Brush

A basting brush is handy for applying marinades or sauces to your dishes. Opt for a silicone or heat-resistant brush that won't melt or shed bristles.

8. Food Prep Tools

Don't forget your basic food prep tools like cutting boards, knives, mixing bowls, and measuring cups and spoons. These essentials are necessary for preparing ingredients before air frying.

9. Oven Mitts or Heat-Resistant Gloves

To protect your hands when removing hot items from the air fryer, use oven mitts or heat-resistant gloves. Safety should always be a top priority in the kitchen.

Having these essential tools and accessories on hand will make your air frying journey more enjoyable and efficient.

Step-by-step guide on how to air fry food:

Step 1: Preheat Your Air Fryer

Start by preheating your air fryer to the desired temperature for your recipe. Most recipes will specify the appropriate temperature. Preheating ensures that your food starts cooking immediately when you place it in the air fryer.

Step 2: Prepare Your Food

While the air fryer is preheating, prepare your food. This includes seasoning, marinating (if necessary), and cutting ingredients into appropriate sizes. Be sure to pat dry any ingredients that are too moist, as excess moisture can affect the crispiness of the food.

Step 3: Arrange Food in the Basket or Tray

Open the air fryer's basket or pull out the tray. Arrange your prepared food items in a single layer. Avoid overcrowding, as this can block the air circulation and result in uneven cooking. If you have a large quantity, you may need to cook in batches.

Step 4: Lightly Coat with Oil (If Desired)

If your recipe calls for it, lightly coat the food with a small amount of cooking oil. You can use a cooking oil spray bottle for even distribution. Remember, air frying uses significantly less oil compared to deep frying.

Step 5: Set Cooking Time and Temperature

Use the control panel or interface of your air fryer to set the cooking time and temperature according to your recipe. Different foods require different settings, so refer to your recipe or air fryer manual for guidance.

Step 6: Start the Air Fryer

Close the air fryer basket or tray, and start the cooking process. The heating element will generate heat, and the fan will circulate hot air around the food.

Step 7: Monitor and Flip (If Necessary)

Keep an eye on your food as it cooks. Depending on the recipe, you may need to pause the air fryer to flip or shake the food halfway through the cooking time. This ensures even browning on all sides.

Step 8: Check for Doneness

Near the end of the cooking time, use a meat thermometer or check the food's internal temperature to ensure it's cooked to the desired level of doneness. Some foods, like poultry, must reach specific internal temperatures for safety.

Step 9: Remove and Serve

Once your food is cooked to perfection, carefully open the air fryer and use silicone-tipped tongs or utensils to remove it. Be cautious as the contents will be hot. Transfer your air-fried creations to a serving plate and enjoy!

Step 10: Clean Your Air Fryer

After you've savored your delicious meal, let your air fryer cool down. Then, clean the basket, tray, and any accessories following the manufacturer's instructions. Most air fryer components are dishwasher safe for easy cleanup.

Proper cleaning and maintenance of your air fryer are essential for its longevity and continued performance. Here's a step-by-step guide on how to clean and maintain your air fryer:

Cleaning Your Air Fryer

• Unplug the Air Fryer: Always make sure your air fryer is unplugged and fully cooled before beginning the cleaning process.

• Remove Removable Parts:Most air fryers come with removable components such as the basket, tray, and pan. Take these out for convenient cleaning.

• Empty the Crumbs:Dispose of any food particles or crumbs from the basket and tray. You can tap them into the trash or use a soft brush to sweep them away.

• Wash Removable Parts: Clean the removable parts with warm, soapy water. Employ a soft sponge or a non-abrasive brush for gentle scrubbing. Avoid abrasive scouring pads, as they can damage the non-stick coating.

• Clean the Inside: Wipe the inside of the air fryer with a damp cloth or sponge. For stubborn residue, a mixture of water and mild detergent can be used. Ensure thorough rinsing and dry with a clean cloth.

• Clean the Heating Element: Use a brush or a soft cloth to delicately clean the heating element or the inside of the air fryer lid. Exercise caution to avoid damaging the heating element.

• Clean the Exterior: Wipe the exterior of the air fryer with a damp cloth. If it's particularly greasy, a mixture of water and mild detergent can be applied. Make sure the exterior is completely dry before plugging it back in.

• Clean the Ventilation System: The ventilation system may accumulate grease and debris over time. Consult your user manual for proper instructions on how to clean it. In certain models, you may be able to remove and wash the air intake and exhaust covers.

Maintaining Your Air Fryer:

• Regular Cleaning: Make it a habit to clean your air fryer after each use. This prevents residue buildup and maintains optimal performance.

• Avoid Abrasives: Avoid using abrasive cleaning materials like steel wool or harsh chemicals, as they can damage the non-stick coating and other parts of the air fryer.

• Check for Wear and Tear: Regularly inspect your air fryer for signs of wear, especially the non-stick coating. If you notice significant damage, it may be time to consider replacing the affected parts or the entire unit.

- Empty the Drip Tray: If your air fryer has a drip tray, make sure to empty it after each use to prevent oil buildup and potential smoke during future cooking.
- Store Properly: Store your air fryer in a clean, dry place when not in use. Avoid stacking heavy items on top of it, as this can damage the appliance.
- Refer to the User Manual: Always follow the manufacturer's instructions for cleaning and maintenance specific to your air fryer model

Neglecting regular maintenance of the air fryer can lead to various issues and diminish its effectiveness. Here are some potential consequences:

- Reduced Performance: Over time, a buildup of food particles, grease, and residue can affect the air fryer's heating element and airflow, resulting in uneven cooking and longer cooking times.
- Food Odors and Flavors: Neglected air fryers may retain food odors and flavors from previous use, affecting the taste of your meals.
- Hygiene Concerns: A lack of cleaning can lead to hygiene issues, including the growth of harmful bacteria, which can compromise your health.
- Safety Hazards: Grease accumulation can become a fire hazard if left unattended for too long, posing a danger to your kitchen and home.

Troubleshooting Your Air Fryer

Encountering issues with your air fryer? Don't worry; we've got solutions to common problems that may arise during your air frying adventures.

Problem: Food is Burnt

- It's easy to overcook food when you're new to air frying. To prevent this, closely monitor your food for doneness. You can safely open the air fryer and check the basket a few times during cooking.

Problem: Food Sticks to the Basket

- To prevent food from sticking to the basket, lightly mist it with olive oil before adding ingredients. Alternatively, use fryer basket parchment liners for added convenience.

Problem: The Air Fryer Produces Smoke

- Smoking can occur when cooking high-fat foods. To minimize smoke, drain excess fat from the bottom of the air fryer during cooking. Placing a tablespoon or two of water under the basket can also reduce smoke while cooking.

Problem: Food Isn't Crispy

- To achieve that perfect crispiness, lightly mist your food with olive oil before cooking. Some recipes benefit from an additional misting midway through the cooking process to enhance crunchiness.

Problem: Sticky or Flaking Basket

- Avoid using aerosol cooking sprays as they can damage the fryer basket over time. Opt for non-aerosol oils to protect your air fryer's components.

Problem: Burnt Plastic Smell

- If your air fryer emits a burnt plastic smell initially, it's often normal and will dissipate after a few uses. If the smell persists, consider contacting the manufacturer for guidance.

By following these troubleshooting tips, you can make the most of your air fryer and enjoy hassle-free cooking experiences.

Foods to eat

Air fryers can be a valuable tool for those looking to lose weight as they allow you to enjoy crispy and flavorful dishes with less oil and fewer calories.

Opt for Lean Proteins

Protein serves as an excellent ally in weight management. Its ability to promote satiety means you're less likely to succumb to snack cravings or overindulge in your next meal. Moreover, protein plays a crucial role in preserving lean muscle mass, further enhancing its benefits.

Embrace Healthy Fats

While fats often get a bad rap, it's essential to distinguish between the harmful and the beneficial kinds. Trans fats and saturated fats are the ones to avoid, especially when aiming for weight loss. On the flip side, healthy fats are vital for energy production, cellular growth, nutrient absorption, and hormone synthesis.

Monounsaturated and polyunsaturated fats are classified as good fats. Common sources include avocados, nuts, seeds, and fish. Opt for oils with lower saturated fat content for a healthier choice.

Prioritize Vegetables

Vegetables are a cornerstone of any effective weight loss plan. They're packed with fiber, water, and essential nutrients, all while boasting lower calorie counts compared to many other foods. Plus, they serve as a dependable source of healthy carbohydrates, contributing to a well-rounded diet.

Here are some healthy foods to eat when using an air fryer for weight loss:

1.   **Lean Proteins:**

- Skinless chicken breasts or thighs

- Turkey breast

- Lean cuts of beef, such as sirloin or tenderloin

- Pork loin or tenderloin

- Fish fillets (salmon, tilapia, cod, etc.)

- Shrimp

2. Vegetables:

- Broccoli

- Cauliflower

- Brussels sprouts

- Asparagus

- Zucchini

- Bell peppers

- Carrot sticks

- Sweet potato fries (in moderation)

- Butternut squash

3. Fruits (in moderation):

- Apples (try making apple chips)

- Pears

- Berries (like strawberries or blueberries)

- Pineapple

4. Whole Grains (sparingly):

- Whole grain tortillas (for making air-fried wraps)

- Whole grain bread for making croutons or breaded coatings (use in moderation)

5. Healthy Snacks:

- Air-fried chickpeas

- Kale chips

- Edamame

- Popcorn (using minimal oil and seasonings)

6. Nuts and Seeds (in moderation):

- Almonds

- Cashews

- Pumpkin seeds

7. Eggs:

- Hard-boiled eggs

- Omelets or scrambled eggs with plenty of veggies

8. Tofu:

- Air-frying tofu can create a crispy texture that's great for salads or stir-fries.

9. Herbs and Spices:

- Experiment with herbs and spices to add flavor without excessive calories. Some popular choices include paprika, garlic powder, cumin, and rosemary.

Remember that portion control is essential for weight loss, even when using an air fryer. While air-frying reduces the need for added oil, it's still important to be mindful of calorie intake.

Foods to Avoid

Certain foods and ingredients should be avoided during your weight loss journey. The recipes in these books exclude these items because, as you'll find, the air fryer can produce satisfying results without them.

Trans fats provide no benefits to your body or overall health. They raise LDL (bad cholesterol) levels and lower HDL (good cholesterol), increasing the risk of heart disease, stroke, and type 2 diabetes. Trans fats are commonly present in processed foods and are labeled as "partially hydrogenated oils" on ingredient lists. Examples of trans fat-rich processed foods include crackers, chips, cookies, cakes, fast food, and vegetable shortening. Hidden sources of trans fat can also be found in items like coffee creamer and baked goods.

While the concept of low-fat foods may seem enticing, it's advisable to steer clear of them unless they are naturally low-fat whole foods. Often, the reduction in fat content in these items is compensated by an increase in sugar. Additionally, these foods may lack flavor, leading to overconsumption.

SCAN

https://sites.google.com/view/freebonusbooks

Your password to open pdf bonus book is:

pdfbonus4u

CHAPTER 2

MEAL PLAN

DAY	BREAKFAST	LUNCH	DINNER
1	Breakfast Pizza	Crispy Onion Rings	Air Fryer Beef and Potato Tacos
2	Green Eggs and Ham	Garlic Roasted Green Beans	Herbed Garlic Butter Turkey Breast
3	Peppered Maple Bacon Knots	Crispy Eggplant Parmesan	Air Fryer Beef and Broccoli
4	Cheddar Soufflés	Teriyaki Glazed Green Beans	Crispy Air Fried Chicken Wings
5	Turkey Breakfast Sausage Patties	Air Fryer Sweet Potato Tots	Air Fryer Beef and Spinach Stuffed Mushrooms
6	Butternut Squash and Ricotta Frittata	Roasted Red Pepper Hummus	Air Fryer Beef and Mushroom Wellington
7	Baked Peach Oatmeal	Stuffed Turkey Peppers	Mediterranean Stuffed Chicken Breast
8	Bacon Cheese Egg with Avocado	Cajun Sweet Potato Wedges	Cajun Spiced Turkey Drumsticks
9	Breakfast Hash	Garlic Parmesan Zucchini Noodles	Rosemary Lemon Cornish Game Hens
10	Savory Sweet Potato Hash	Air Fryer Coconut Shrimp	Air Fryer Beef and Onion Stuffed Potatoes
11	Cheddar Eggs	Caprese Stuffed Portobello Mushrooms	Pesto and Mozzarella Stuffed Turkey Meatballs
12	Southwestern Ham Egg Cups	Air Fryer Bruschetta	Air Fryer Lamb Samosas
13	Breakfast Sausage and Cauliflower	Stuffed Mushrooms with Crab	Coconut Curry Chicken
14	Spinach and Bacon Roll-ups	Stuffed Mushrooms with Spinach and Cheese	Pork and Mushroom Risotto
15	Jalapeño and Bacon Breakfast Pizza	Crispy Broccoli Tots	Pork and Apple Stuffed Acorn Squash

16	Buffalo Egg Cups	Butternut Squash Fries	Cajun Blackened Turkey Breast
17	Canadian Bacon Muffin Sandwiches	Sweet and Spicy Carrot Fries	Moroccan Lamb Skewers
18	Classic British Breakfast	Taco-Spiced Chickpeas	Pork and Pineapple Tacos
19	Bacon and Cheese Quiche	Coconut-Crusted Sweet Potato Fries	Lamb and Vegetable Stir-Fry
20	Smoky Sausage Patties	Garlic Butter Mushrooms	Crispy Lemon Pepper Chicken Wings
21	Cheesy Bell Pepper Eggs	Lemon Herb Roasted Potatoes	Pork and Vegetable Spring Rolls
22	Poached Eggs on Whole Grain Avocado Toast	Parmesan Roasted Broccoli	Spicy Buffalo Chicken Bites
23	Golden Avocado Tempura	Corn on the Cob	Pork and Sweet Potato Hash
24	Asparagus and Bell Pepper Strata	Balsamic-Glazed Brussel Sprouts	Pork and Bean Burritos
25	Crispy Broccoli Tots	Crispy Eggplant Parmesan	Garlic Parmesan Chicken Tenders
26	Strawberry Toast	Garlic Herb Roasted Potatoes	Honey Mustard Glazed Chicken Thighs
27	Whole Wheat Banana-Walnut Bread	Garlic Roasted Green Beans	Paprika-Rubbed Air Fryer Chicken
28	Green Eggs and Ham	Air Fryer Garlic Parmesan Asparagus	Lemon Herb Roast Chicken
29	Kale and Potato Nuggets	Asparagus with Lemon and Parmesan	White Fish with Cauliflower
30	Sausage Egg Cup	Air Fryer Ratatouille	BBQ Chicken Drumsticks

CHAPTER 3

BREAKFAST RECIPES

Breakfast Pita

Prep time: 5 mins   Cook time: 6 mins
Serves 2
Ingredients
¼ teaspoon garlic, minced
⅛ teaspoon salt
1 large egg
¼ teaspoon dried oregano
1 whole wheat pita
2 teaspoons olive oil
½ shallot, diced
¼ teaspoon dried thyme
2 tablespoons shredded Parmesan cheese

Directions
Set the air fryer's temperature to 380°F.
After brushing the top with olive oil, spread the minced garlic and shallot over the pita. Crack the egg into a small bowl or ramekin, and season it with oregano, thyme, and salt.
Put the pita in the air fryer basket, and then carefully pour the egg on top of it. Cheese should be added on top. Bake for 6 mins.
Before chopping into pieces for serving, let the food cool for five minutes.

Nutritional Values (per serving): Calories: 282 Fat: 15g Carbohydrates: 25g Protein: 12g

Turkey Breakfast Sausage Patties

Prep time: 5 mins   Cook time: 10 mins
Serves 4
Ingredients
¾ teaspoon smoked paprika

½ teaspoon onion powder
½ teaspoon garlic powder
1 pound (454 g) 93% lean ground turkey
½ cup finely minced sweet apple (peeled)
1 tablespoon chopped fresh thyme
1 tablespoon chopped fresh sage
1¼ teaspoons kosher salt
1 teaspoon chopped fennel seeds
⅛ teaspoon crushed red pepper flakes
⅛ teaspoon freshly ground black pepper

Directions
Combine the thyme, sage, salt, fennel seeds, paprika, onion powder, garlic powder, red pepper flakes, and black pepper thoroughly in a medium-sized mixing bowl. Next, add the ground turkey and apple to the spice mixture, stirring until everything is well blended. Divide the resulting mixture into 8 equally sized portions and shape them into patties, each approximately ¼ inch thick and 3 inches in diameter. Preheat your air fryer to 400ºF (204ºC). Arrange the patties in a single layer within the air fryer basket. Depending on the size of your basket, you may need to work in batches to ensure they cook evenly.
Air-fry the patties for 5 minutes, then carefully flip them and air fry for an additional 5 minutes or until they achieve a beautiful golden-brown color and are thoroughly cooked.
Remove the patties from the air fryer basket and place them on a plate. Repeat the process with any remaining patties.
Serve the patties while still warm and enjoy!

Nutritional Values (per serving): Calories: 184 Fat: 10g Carbohydrates: 4g Protein: 16g

Breakfast Sausage and Cauliflower

Prep time: 5 mins   Cook time: 45 mins
Serves 4
Ingredients
1 pound (454 g) sausage, cooked and crumbled
2 cups heavy whipping cream
1 head cauliflower, chopped
1 cup grated Cheddar cheese, plus more for topping
8 eggs, beaten
Salt and ground black pepper, to taste

Directions
Begin by preheating your air fryer to 350ºF (177ºC).
In a bowl bowl, combine the sausage, heavy whipping cream, chopped cauliflower, cheese, and eggs. Season the mixture with salt and ground black pepper to taste. Grease a casserole dish and pour the mixture into it.
Bake the casserole in the preheated air fryer for approximately 45 mins, or until it becomes firm and thoroughly cooked.
Sprinkle some more Cheddar cheese on top of the casserole before serving.
Nutritional Values (per serving): Calories: 361 Fat: 20g Carbs: 20g Protein: 24g

Breakfast Hash

Prep time: 10 mins   Cook time: 30 mins
Serves 6
Ingredients
Oil, for spraying
1 teaspoon salt
½ teaspoon freshly ground black pepper
2 tablespoons olive oil
2 teaspoons granulated garlic
3 medium russet potatoes, diced
½ yellow onion, diced
1 green bell pepper, seeded and diced
Directions
Prepare your air fryer basket. Line it with parchment paper and give it a light coating of cooking oil spray.
In a big bowl, combine the potatoes, onions, bell peppers, and olive oil. Ensure that all the ingredients are thoroughly mixed.

Add the garlic, salt, and black pepper to the mixture, stirring until everything is evenly coated.
Transfer the prepared mixture into the lined and oiled air fryer basket.
Set your air fryer to 400ºF (204ºC) and cook for approximately 20 to 30 minutes. Remember to shake or stir the contents every 10 minutes to ensure even cooking and browning.
For that extra crunch and flavor, consider spraying the potatoes lightly with oil each time you stir them during cooking. This will result in an even crispier texture.
Nutritional Values (per serving): Calories: 242 Fat: 10g Carbs: 30g Protein: 7g

Breakfast Pizza

Prep time: 5 mins   Cook time: 8 mins
Serves 1
Ingredients
2 large eggs
¼ cup unsweetened, unflavored almond milk (or unflavored hemp milk for nut-free)
¼ teaspoon fine sea salt
⅛ teaspoon ground black pepper
¼ cup diced onions
¼ cup shredded Parmesan cheese (omit for dairy-free)
6 pepperoni slices (omit for vegetarian)
¼ teaspoon dried oregano leaves
¼ cup pizza sauce, warmed, for serving

Directions
Preheat the air fryer to 350ºF (177ºC). Carefully grease a cake pan.
Combine the salt, eggs, almond milk, and pepper in a small bowl using a fork. Add the onions and stir well.
Pour the prepared mixture into the greased pan. Top with the cheese, pepperoni slices, and oregano.
Place the pan in the air fryer and bake the mixture for 8 mins, or until the eggs are cooked to your preferred level of doneness.
Gently release the edges of the eggs from the sides of the pan using a spatula, then transfer the egg dish onto a serving plate.
Drizzle pizza sauce over the top just before serving.
Nutritional Values (per serving): Calories: 185 Fat: 11g Carbs: 10g Protein: 12g

Bacon and Cheese Quiche

Prep time: 5 mins   Cook time: 12 mins
Serves 2
Ingredients
¼ teaspoon salt
4 slices cooked sugar-free bacon, crumbled
½ cup shredded mild Cheddar cheese
3 large eggs
2 tablespoons heavy whipping cream

Directions
In a large bowl, combine cream, eggs, and salt together until well mixed. Add bacon and Cheddar.
Pour mixture evenly into two ungreased ramekins. Place into air fryer basket, then preheat the temperature to 320ºF (160ºC).
Bake the mixture for 12 mins, or until the Quiche is fluffy and set in the middle when done. Let it cool in ramekins for 5 mins, then serve warm.
Nutritional Values (per serving): Calories: 226 Fat: 15g Carbs: 10g Protein: 14g

Buffalo Egg Cups

Prep time: 10 mins   Cook time: 15 mins
Serves 2
Ingredients
4 large eggs
2 ounces (57 g) full-fat cream cheese
2 tablespoons buffalo sauce
½ cup shredded sharp Cheddar cheese

Directions
Break the eggs into two ramekins.
Combine the cream cheese, buffalo sauce, and Cheddar eggs in a microwave-safe container. Microwave the mixture for 20 seconds and then stir. Place a spoonful of the mixture into each ramekin on top of the eggs.
Put ramekins in the air fryer basket, then preheat the temperature to 320ºF (160ºC) and bake for 15 mins. Serve and enjoy.
Nutritional Values (per serving): Calories: 213 Fat: 14g Carbs: 12g Fiber: 1g Protein: 15g

Baked Peach Oatmeal

Prep time: 5 mins   Cook time: 30 mins
Serves 6
Ingredients
¼ cup raw honey, plus more for drizzling (optional)
½ cup nonfat plain Greek yogurt
1 teaspoon vanilla extract
¼ teaspoon salt
1½ cups diced peaches, divided, plus more for serving (optional)
Olive oil cooking spray
2 cups certified gluten-free rolled oats
2 cups unsweetened almond milk
½ teaspoon ground cinnamon

Directions
Preheat your air fryer to 380°F (193ºC). Gently apply a thin layer of olive oil cooking spray to the interior of a 6-inch cake pan.
In a big mixing bowl, blend the oats, almond milk, honey, yogurt, vanilla, cinnamon, and a pinch of salt until they are thoroughly combined. Add ¾ cup of the diced peaches, then transfer the mixture into the prepared cake pan. Scatter the remaining peaches evenly over the oatmeal mixture.
Air fry for 30 mins, allowing it to cook to your desired level of doneness. Afterward, let it rest and cool for 5 mins before serving. If desired, enhance the dish with extra peaches and a drizzle of honey.
Nutritional Values (per serving): Calories: 251 Fat: 6g Carbs: 40g Fiber: 5g Protein: 10g

Poached Eggs on Whole Grain Avocado Toast

Prep time: 5 mins   Cook time: 7 mins
Serves 4
Ingredients
Black pepper
4 pieces whole grain bread
Olive oil cooking spray
4 large eggs
Salt to taste
1 avocado
Red pepper flakes (optional)

Directions
Preheat your air fryer to 320°F (160ºC). Apply a light coating of olive oil cooking spray to the interior of four small oven-safe ramekins.
Carefully crack one egg into each ramekin, and season them with a pinch of salt and a dash of black pepper.
Position the ramekins in the air fryer basket, close the lid, and set the timer for 7 minutes.
While the eggs are cooking, toast the bread in a toaster until it reaches your desired level of crispness.
Take an avocado, slice it in half lengthwise, remove the pit, and scoop the creamy flesh into a small bowl. Season it with salt, black pepper, and red pepper, if desired. Using a fork, lightly mash the avocado.
Spread a quarter of the mashed avocado evenly over each slice of toast.
Once the eggs are done in the air fryer, carefully remove them and gently place one on top of each slice of avocado toast before serving.
Nutritional Values (per serving): Calories: 274 Fat: 14g Carbs: 25g Fiber: 4g Protein: 15g

Cheddar Eggs

Prep time: 5 mins Cook time: 15 mins
Serves 2
Ingredients
2 tablespoons unsalted butter, melted
4 large eggs

½ cup shredded sharp Cheddar cheese
Directions
Break the eggs into a round baking dish and whisk thoroughly.
Place dish into the air fryer basket, then set the temperature to 400ºF (204ºC) and also the timer for 10 mins.
After 5 mins, stir the eggs and add the butter and cheese. Allow it to cook 3 additional mins and stir again.
Let the eggs to finish cooking an additional 2 mins or remove if they are to your desired level of doneness. Use a fork to fluff, then serve warm.
Nutritional Values (per serving): Calories: 228 Fat: 14g Carbs: 8g Fiber: 1g Protein: 15g

Peppered Maple Bacon Knots

Prep time: 5 mins   Cook time: 7 to 8 mins
Serves 6
Ingredients
¼ cup brown sugar
Coarsely cracked black peppercorns, to taste
1 pound (454 g) maple smoked center-cut bacon
¼ cup maple syrup

Directions
Preheat the air fryer to 390ºF (199ºC).
Tie each bacon strip in a loose knot.
Combine the maple syrup and brown sugar in a small bowl. Brush this mixture over the bacon knots.
Place the bacon knots in the air fryer basket, then season with the coarsely cracked black peppercorns.
Air fry for 5 mins. Turn the bacon knots to another side, then cook for another 2 to 3 mins, or until the bacon is crisp.
Remove the bacon from the basket to a paper towel-lined plate.
Repeat the process for the remaining bacon knots.
Nutritional Values (per serving): Calories: 282 Fat: 20g Carbs: 13g Fiber: 1g Protein: 12g

Smoky Sausage Patties

Prep time: 30 mins   Cook time: 9 mins
Serves 8
Ingredients
½ teaspoon dried thyme
½ teaspoon freshly ground black pepper
¼ teaspoon cayenne pepper
1 teaspoon dried sage
1 teaspoon sea salt
1 pound (454 g) ground pork
1 tablespoon coconut aminos
2 teaspoons liquid smoke
½ teaspoon fennel seeds

Directions

In a clean bowl, mix together the pork, coconut aminos, liquid smoke, sage, salt, fennel seeds, thyme, black pepper, and cayenne pepper. Use your hands to blend the seasonings thoroughly into the meat.

Form the mixture into 8 evenly sized patties. Create a slight point in the center of each patty using your thumb. Arrange the patties on a plate and cover them with plastic wrap. Let the patties chill in the refrigerator for a minimum of 30 minutes.

If needed, work in batches to ensure the patties are in a single layer in the air fryer, avoiding overcrowding.

Set the air fryer to 400ºF (204ºC) and air fry for 5 minutes. Flip the patties and continue cooking for approximately 4 more minutes.
Nutritional Values (per serving): Calories: 241 Fat: 16g Carbs: 3g Fiber: 0g Protein: 18g

Spinach and Bacon Roll-ups

Prep time: 5 mins   Cook time: 8 to 9 mins
Serves 4
Ingredients
4 flour tortillas (6- or 7-inch size)
4 slices Swiss cheese
1 cup baby spinach leaves
4 slices turkey bacon
Special Equipment: 4 toothpicks, soak in water for at least 30 mins

Directions

Preheat the air fryer to 390ºF (199ºC).

Lay out each tortilla on a clean work surface and place a slice of cheese and ¼ cup of spinach on top of each one. Roll them tightly.

Wrap each tortilla with a strip of turkey bacon and secure it with a toothpick.

Place the roll-ups in the air fryer basket, ensuring there's space between each one.

Air fry for 4 minutes, then use tongs to flip the roll-ups and rearrange them for even cooking. Continue air frying for an additional 4 to 5 minutes until the bacon becomes crispy.

Allow the roll-ups to rest for 5 minutes, then remove the toothpicks before serving. Enjoy!
Nutritional Values (per serving): Calories: 239 Fat: 14g Carbs: 20g Fiber: 2g Protein: 12g

Strawberry Toast

Prep time: 10 mins   Cook time: 8 mins
Makes 4 toasts
Ingredients
4 slices bread, ½-inch thick
Butter-flavored cooking spray
1 cup sliced strawberries
1 teaspoon sugar

Directions

Spray one side of each bread slice with butter-flavored cooking spray, then place them with the sprayed side facing down.

Distribute the strawberries evenly among the bread slices. Sprinkle the sugar evenly over the strawberries.

Arrange the prepared slices in a single layer in the air fryer basket.

Air fry at 390ºF (199ºC) for 8 minutes until the bottom becomes brown and crisp, and the top has a glazed appearance. Enjoy your strawberry toast!
Nutritional Values (per serving): Calories: 185 Fat: 4g Carbs: 25g Fiber: 3g Protein: 5g

Golden Avocado Tempura

Prep time: 5 mins   **Cook time: 10 mins**
Serves 4
Ingredients
½ cup bread crumbs
½ teaspoons salt
1 Haas avocado, pitted, peeled and sliced
Liquid from 1 can white beans

Directions
Heat up the air fryer to 350ºF (177ºC).
Combine the bread crumbs and salt in a deep bowl, ensuring they are well mixed.
Dip the avocado slices into the bean liquid and then coat them with the bread crumbs.
Place the avocado slices in the air fryer, making sure not to overlap them. Air fry for 10 minutes, shaking the basket halfway through the cooking time. Serve your crispy avocado slices immediately.
Nutritional Values (per serving): Calories: 150 Fat: 10g Carbs: 9g Fiber: 4g Protein: 4g

Sausage Egg Cup

Prep time: 10 mins   **Cook time: 15 mins**
Serves 6
Ingredients
12 ounces (340 g) ground pork breakfast sausage
6 large eggs
½ teaspoon salt
¼ teaspoon ground black pepper
½ teaspoon crushed red pepper flakes

Directions
Grease six 4-inch ramekins (approximately 2 ounces / 57g per ramekin) with cooking oil. Place sausage in each ramekin, pressing it down to cover the bottom and extend about ½-inch up the sides of the ramekins. Crack one egg into each ramekin and evenly sprinkle with salt, black pepper, and red pepper flakes.

Arrange the ramekins in the air fryer basket. Adjust the temperature to 350ºF (177ºC) and set the timer for 15 minutes. The egg cups will be ready when the sausage is fully cooked to at least 145ºF (63ºC), and the egg is firm.
Serve the delicious egg and sausage cups while they're still warm. Enjoy!
Nutritional Values (per serving): Calories: 163 Fat: 10g Carbs: 7g Fiber: 1g Protein: 12g

Pancake Cake

Prep time: 10 mins   **Cook time: 7 mins**
Serves 4
Ingredients
½ cup blanched finely ground almond flour
¼ cup powdered erythritol
½ teaspoon baking powder
2 tablespoons unsalted butter, softened
1 large egg
½ teaspoon unflavored gelatin
½ teaspoon vanilla extract
½ teaspoon ground cinnamon

Directions
Combine almond flour, erythritol, and baking powder in a large bowl. Add in the butter, egg, gelatin, vanilla, and cinnamon, then pour the mixture into a round baking pan.
Carefully place the pan into the air fryer basket. Heat up the air fryer to 300ºF (149ºC) and set the timer for 7 minutes.
4. To check if the cake is fully cooked, put a toothpick into it; if it comes out clean, the cake is done. Then, cut the cake into four portions and serve.
Nutritional Values (per serving): Calories: 151 Fat: 10g Carbs: 15g Fiber: 3g Protein: 3g

Cheddar Soufflés

Prep time: 15 mins   Cook time: 12 mins
Serves 4
Ingredients
3 large eggs, whites and yolks separated
¼ teaspoon cream of tartar
½ cup shredded sharp Cheddar cheese
3 ounces (85 g) cream cheese, softened
Directions
In a large bowl, beat the egg whites along with the cream of tartar until soft peaks form, which should take about 2 minutes.
In a separate medium-sized bowl, beat the egg yolks, Cheddar cheese, and cream cheese until the mixture becomes frothy, approximately 1 minute. Gently fold the egg yolk mixture into the beaten egg whites until well combined.
Grease four ramekins with cooking spray and pour the mixture evenly into them. Place the ramekins in the air fryer basket.
Adjust the air fryer temperature to 350ºF (177ºC) and bake for 12 minutes. The eggs should have a browned top and a firm center when they are done. Serve!!!
Nutritional Values (per serving): Calories: 129 Fat: 7g Carbs: 7g Fiber: 0g Protein: 10g

Savory Sweet Potato Hash

Prep time: 15 mins Cook time: 18 mins
Serves 6
Ingredients
2 medium sweet potatoes, peeled and cut into 1-inch cubes
½ green bell pepper, diced
½ red onion, diced
4 ounces (113 g) baby bella mushrooms, diced
2 tablespoons olive oil
1 garlic clove, minced
½ teaspoon salt
½ teaspoon black pepper
½ tablespoon chopped fresh rosemary
Directions
Preheat the air fryer to 380°F(193ºC). In a large bowl, combine all the ingredients together until the vegetables are thoroughly coated and the seasonings are evenly distributed.

Pour the prepared vegetables into the air fryer basket, ensuring they form a single, even layer. If you're using a smaller air fryer, you might need to do this in two batches.
Roast the vegetables for 9 mins, then toss or flip them. Roast for another 9 mins. Pour the roasted vegetables into a serving bowl or individual plates, and serve.
Nutritional Values (per serving): Calories: 174 Fat: 9g Carbs: 23g Fiber: 4g Protein: 4g

Butternut Squash and Ricotta Frittata

Prep time: 10 mins   Cook time: 33 mins
Serves 2 to 3
Ingredients
1 cup cubed (½-inch) butternut squash (5½ ounces / 156 g)
2 tablespoons olive oil
Kosher salt and freshly ground black pepper, to taste
4 fresh sage leaves, thinly sliced
6 large eggs, lightly beaten
½ cup ricotta cheese
Cayenne pepper
Directions
Combine the squash with olive oil in a bowl, season it with salt and black pepper for an even coating. Spread sage in the bottom of a cake pan, then arrange the squash on top. Position the pan inside the air fryer and cook at 400ºF (204ºC) for 10 minutes. Mix to blend in the sage, then continue cooking until the squash becomes tender and lightly caramelized at the edges, which should take about 3 minutes more. Next, pour the eggs over the squash, distribute dollops of ricotta evenly, and sprinkle with cayenne. Bake in the air fryer at 300ºF (149ºC) until the eggs set and the frittata turns golden brown on top, approximately 20 minutes. Once done, remove the pan from the air fryer and cut the frittata into wedges for serving.
Nutritional Values (per serving): Calories: 282 Fat: 13g Carbs: 20g Fiber: 4g Protein: 16g

Jalapeño and Bacon Breakfast Pizza

Prep time: 5 mins Cook time: 10 mins
Serves 2
Ingredients
4 slices cooked sugar-free bacon, chopped
¼ cup chopped pickled jalapeños
1 large egg, whisked
1 cup shredded Mozzarella cheese
1 ounce (28 g) cream cheese, broken into small pieces
¼ teaspoon salt

Directions
Arrange Mozzarella evenly at the base of an ungreased circular nonstick baking dish. Spread cream cheese chunks, bacon, and jalapeños across the Mozzarella, followed by an even pouring of the egg around the dish.
Add a dash of salt, then transfer it to the air fryer basket. Set the temperature to 330ºF (166ºC) and cook for 10 minutes. The pizza will be ready when the cheese is golden and the egg has solidified.
Allow it to cool on a large plate for 5 minutes before serving.
Nutritional Values (per serving): Calories: 237 Fat: 15g Carbs: 15g Fiber: 1g Protein: 12g

Bacon Cheese Egg with Avocado

Prep time: 15 mins   Cook   time: 20 mins Serves 4
Ingredients
6 large eggs
¼ cup heavy whipping cream
1½ cups chopped cauliflower
1 cup shredded medium Cheddar cheese
1 medium avocado, peeled and pitted
12 slices sugar-free bacon, cooked and crumbled
8 tablespoons full-fat sour cream
2 scallions, sliced on the bias

Directions
Combine eggs and cream in a medium-sized bowl. Empty the mixture into a circular baking dish.
Add cauliflower and then combine together, then layer it with Cheddar. Position the dish inside the air fryer basket. Set the temperature to 320ºF (160ºC) and time it for 20 minutes.
Once fully cooked, the eggs will be solid, and the cheese will be nicely browned. Slice it into four portions. Cut avocado into slices and distribute them evenly among the portions. Finish each piece with 2 tablespoons of sour cream, sliced scallions, and crumbled bacon.
Nutritional Values (per serving): Calories: 374 Fat: 25g Carbs: 15g Fiber: 3g Protein: 20g

Classic British Breakfast

Prep time: 5 mins   Cook time: 25 mins
Serves 2
Ingredients
2 eggs
1 tablespoon olive oil
Salt, to taste
1 sausage
1 cup potatoes, sliced and diced
2 cups beans in tomato sauce

Directions
Preheat the air fryer to 390ºF (199ºC) until it's thoroughly heated.
Crack the eggs onto a baking dish and add a pinch of salt.
Position the beans beside the eggs in the dish.
Coat the potatoes with olive oil in a bowl and sprinkle with salt.
Place the bowl of potato slices in the air fryer and cook for 10 minutes.
Afterward, replace the potato bowl with the dish holding the eggs and beans. Continue baking for an additional 10 minutes, covering the potatoes with parchment paper.
Slice the sausage and place the slices on top of the beans and eggs. Bake for an extra 5 minutes. Serve alongside the potatoes.
Nutritional Values (per serving): Calories: 450 Fat: 23g Carbs: 25g Fiber: 5g Protein: 20g

Southwestern Ham Egg Cups

Prep time: 5 mins   Cook time: 12 mins
Serves 2
Ingredients
¼ cup diced green bell pepper
2 tablespoons diced white onion
½ cup shredded medium Cheddar cheese
2 tablespoons diced red bell pepper
4 (1-ounce / 28-g) slices deli ham
4 large eggs
2 tablespoons full-fat sour cream

Directions
Put a single ham slice at the base of each of the four baking cups.
In a big bowl, combine eggs with sour cream. Add green pepper, red pepper, and onion.
Empty the egg mixture into the baking cups lined with ham. Sprinkle Cheddar on top. Then, put the cups in the air fryer basket.
Set the temperature to 320ºF (160ºC) and cook for approximately 12 minutes, or until the tops become golden brown. Enjoy while it's warm.
Nutritional Values (per serving): Calories: 273 Fat: 15g Carbs: 15g Protein: 18g

Whole Wheat Banana-Walnut Bread

Prep time: 10 mins   Cook time: 23 mins
Serves 6
Ingredients
¼ cup nonfat plain Greek yogurt
1 cup whole wheat flour
¼ teaspoon salt
¼ teaspoon baking soda
¼ cup olive oil
½ teaspoon vanilla extract
Olive oil cooking spray
2 ripe medium bananas
1 large egg
2 tablespoons raw honey
½ teaspoon ground cinnamon
¼ cup chopped walnuts

Directions
Preheat the air fryer to 360°F (182ºC). Lightly apply olive oil cooking spray to the interior of an 8-by-4-inch loaf pan. (Alternatively, you can use two 5 ½-by-3-inch loaf pans.)
Mash the bananas in a large bowl using a fork. Add the egg, yogurt, olive oil, vanilla, and honey. Combine thoroughly until mostly smooth. Sieve the whole wheat flour, salt, baking soda, and cinnamon into the wet mixture, then gently stir until just blended. Avoid overmixing. Carefully add the walnuts.
Pour the mixture into the prepared loaf pan, ensuring an even distribution.
Position the loaf pan in the air fryer basket and bake for 20 to 23 minutes, or until the top is golden brown, and a toothpick inserted into the center comes out clean.
Allow to cool for 5 minutes before serving.
Nutritional Values (per serving): Calories: 240 Fat: 8g Carbs: 33g Protein: 5g

Cheesy Bell Pepper Eggs

Prep time: 10 mins   Cook time: 15 mins
Serves 4
Ingredients
4 medium green bell peppers
3 ounces (85 g) cooked ham, chopped
¼ medium onion, peeled and chopped
8 large eggs
1 cup mild Cheddar cheese

Directions
First, trim the tops of each bell pepper and remove the seeds and white membranes using a small knife. Fill each pepper with ham and onion.
Crack two eggs into each pepper and top them with ¼ cup of cheese per pepper. Place the stuffed peppers into the air fryer basket.
Adjust the temperature to 390ºF (199ºC) and air fry for 15 minutes.
Once fully cooked, the peppers will be tender, and the eggs will be firm. Serve immediately.
Nutritional Values (per serving): Calories: 264 Fat: 16g Carbs: 15g Protein: 17g

Asparagus and Bell Pepper Strata

Prep time: 10 mins Cook time: 14 to 20 mins
Serves 4
Ingredients
2 slices low-sodium whole-wheat bread, cut into ½-inch cubes
3 tablespoons 1% milk
½ teaspoon dried thyme
3 egg whites
8 large asparagus spears, trimmed and cut into 2-inch pieces
$1/_3$ cup shredded carrot
½ cup chopped red bell pepper
1 egg

Directions
Combine the asparagus, carrot, red bell pepper, and 1 tablespoon of water in a baking pan. Bake them in the air fryer at 330ºF (166ºC) for 3 to 5 minutes, or until they reach a crisp-tender texture. Make sure to drain them thoroughly.
Toss the bread cubes with the vegetables gently.
In a medium-sized bowl, whisk together the egg whites, egg, milk, and thyme until the mixture becomes frothy.
Pour the egg mixture into the pan and bake for 11 to 15 minutes, or until the strata becomes slightly puffy, sets, and the top begins to brown. Then, serve.
Nutritional Values (per serving): Calories: 221 Fat: 6g Carbs: 25g Protein: 12g

Canadian Bacon Muffin Sandwiches

Prep time: 5 mins   Cook time: 8 mins
Serves 4
Ingredients
4 slices cheese
Cooking spray
4 English muffins, split
8 slices Canadian bacon

Directions
Heat up the air fryer to 370ºF (188ºC).
Make the sandwiches by placing 2 slices of Canadian bacon and 1 slice of cheese on each of the 4 muffin halves, then top them with the remaining muffin halves.
Arrange the sandwiches in the air fryer basket and lightly spray the tops with cooking spray.
Air fry for 4 minutes, then flip the sandwiches and cook for an additional 4 minutes.
Serve the warm sandwiches evenly on four plates.
Nutritional Values (per serving): Calories: 290 Fat: 16g Carbs: 28g Protein: 12g

Kale and Potato Nuggets

Prep time: 10 mins   Cook time: 18 mins
Serves 4
Ingredients
1 teaspoon extra virgin olive oil
1 clove garlic, minced
4 cups kale, rinsed and chopped
2 cups potatoes, boiled and mashed
⅛ cup milk
Salt and ground black pepper, to taste
Cooking spray

Directions
Preheat the air fryer to 390ºF (199ºC).
Heat garlic in olive oil in a skillet over medium heat until it achieves a golden-brown color. Stir in the kale for an additional 3 minutes, then remove from heat.
Combine mashed potatoes, sautéed kale, and garlic in a bowl. Add milk and season with salt and pepper.
Form the mixture into nugget shapes and lightly coat them with cooking spray.
Place the nuggets into the air fryer basket and air fry for 15 minutes. Remember to flip the nuggets halfway through cooking to ensure even frying. Serve immediately.
Nutritional Values (per serving): Calories: 175 Fat: 9g Carbs: 16g Protein: 7g

Johnny Cakes

Prep time: 10 mins   Cook time: 10 to 12 mins
Serves 4
Ingredients
1 teaspoon baking powder
1 tablespoon butter, melted
1 large egg, lightly beaten
1 to 2 tablespoons oil
1 teaspoon salt
½ cup all-purpose flour
1½ cups yellow cornmeal
2 tablespoons sugar
1 cup milk, whole or 2%
Directions
Mix the flour, cornmeal, sugar, baking powder, and salt in a large bowl until they're well blended. Add milk, melted butter, and egg to create a mixture that's sticky but still has some lumps.
Preheat the air fryer to 350ºF (177ºC) and place parchment paper in the air fryer basket.
Drop 1 heaping tablespoon of batter onto the parchment paper to create each cake. You should be able to put 4 cakes in the fryer.
Apply a spritz of oil to the cakes and cook for 3 minutes. Then, flip the cakes, add another spritz of oil, and cook for an additional 2 to 3 minutes. Repeat this process for a second batch of cakes
Nutritional Values (per serving): Calories: 150 Fat: 4g Carbs: 25g Protein: 3g

Gluten-Free Granola Cereal

Prep time: 7 mins   Cook time: 30 mins
Makes 3½ cups
Ingredients
1 tablespoon toasted sesame oil or vegetable oil
1 teaspoon ground cinnamon
½ cup chopped almonds
½ cup pumpkin seeds
¼ cup maple syrup or honey
Oil, for spraying
1½ cups gluten-free rolled oats
½ cup chopped walnuts
½ teaspoon salt
½ cup dried cranberries

Directions
Preheat the air fryer to 250ºF (121ºC). Line the air fryer basket with parchment paper and lightly apply oil. (Ensure you line the basket; the parchment prevents the granola from falling through the holes.)
In a spacious bowl, combine oats, walnuts, almonds, pumpkin seeds, maple syrup, sesame oil, cinnamon, and salt.
Spread this mixture evenly in the prepared basket. Cook for 30 minutes, stirring every 10 minutes. Transfer the granola to a bowl, add the dried cranberries, and mix properly.
Allow the granola to cool to room temperature before storing it in an airtight container.
Nutritional Values (per serving): Calories: 190 Fat: 7g Carbs: 27g Protein: 4g

Green Eggs and Ham

Prep time: 5 mins   Cook time: 10 mins
Serves 2
Ingredients
2 tablespoons chopped green onions, plus more for garnish
¼ cup shredded Cheddar cheese (omit for dairy-free)
½ teaspoon fine sea salt
¼ teaspoon ground black pepper
1 large Hass avocado, halved and pitted
2 thin slices ham
2 large eggs
Directions
Heat up the air fryer to 400ºF (204ºC).
In each avocado half, put a slice of ham. Crack an egg over the ham and then add a sprinkle of green onions, salt, and pepper.
Arrange the avocado halves in the air fryer with the cut side facing up and air fry for 10 minutes or until the egg reaches your preferred level of doneness. If you're using cheese, top the avocados with it and air fry for an additional 30 seconds, or until the cheese melts. Finish by garnishing with chopped green onions. It's best served fresh.
Nutritional Values (per serving): Calories: 250 Fat: 13g Carbs: 20g Protein: 14g

CHAPTER 4
FISH AND SEAFOOD RECIPES

Honey-Glazed Salmon

Prep time: 5 mins   **Cook time: 12 mins**
Serves 4
Ingredients
½ teaspoon salt
Olive oil cooking spray
4 (1½-inch-thick) salmon fillets
¼ cup raw honey
4 garlic cloves, minced
1 tablespoon olive oil

Directions
Heat the air fryer to 380°F (193ºC).
Combine honey, garlic, olive oil, and salt in a small bowl.
Coat the underside of the air fryer basket with olive oil cooking spray, and arrange the salmon in a single layer at the basket's base.
Apply the honey-garlic mixture to the upper side of each fillet, then cook for 10 to 12 minutes, or until the internal temperature reaches 145°F (63ºC).
Nutritional Values (per serving): Calories: 240 Fat: 14g Carbs: 10g Protein: 20g

Oregano Tilapia Fingers

Prep time: 15 mins   **Cook time: 9 mins**
Serves 4
Ingredients
½ teaspoon ground paprika
1 teaspoon dried oregano
1 teaspoon avocado oil
1 pound (454 g) tilapia fillet
½ cup coconut flour
2 eggs, beaten

Directions
Slice the tilapia fillets into strips and season with ground paprika and dried oregano.

Next, put the tilapia strips in beaten eggs and brush them with coconut flour.
Drizzle the fish strips with avocado oil and air fry at 370ºF (188ºC) for 9 minutes.
Nutritional Values (per serving): Calories: 162 Fat: 5g Carbs: 10g Protein: 20g

Crispy Herbed Salmon

Prep time: 5 mins   **Cook time: 9 to 12 mins**
Serves 4
Ingredients
½ teaspoon dried basil
$^1/_3$ cup crushed potato chips
2 tablespoons olive oil
¼ cup panko bread crumbs
4 (6-ounce / 170-g) skinless salmon fillets
3 tablespoons honey mustard
½ teaspoon dried thyme

Directions
Put the salmon on a plate. In a small dish, thoroughly combine the mustard, thyme, and basil, then distribute it evenly over the salmon. In another clean bowl, mix the breadcrumbs and potato chips thoroughly. Drizzle with olive oil and stir until it's well combined.
Position the salmon in the air fryer basket and gently, yet firmly, press the breadcrumb mixture onto the surface of each fillet.
Air fry at 320ºF (160ºC) for 9 to 12 minutes or until the salmon's internal temperature reaches at least 145ºF (63ºC) on a meat thermometer, and the topping becomes golden and crispy.
Nutritional Values (per serving): Calories: 227 Fat: 11g Carbs: 10g Protein: 23g

Cajun Salmon

Prep time: 5 mins   Cook time: 7 mins
Serves 2
Ingredients
⅛ teaspoon ground cayenne pepper
1 teaspoon paprika
¼ teaspoon ground black pepper
½ teaspoon garlic powder
2 (4-ounce / 113-g) salmon fillets, skin removed
2 tablespoons unsalted butter, melted

Directions
Apply butter to each fillet.
Mix the remaining components in a compact dish and then massage them onto the fish. Put the fillets into the air fryer basket.
Set the temperature to 390ºF (199ºC) and air fry for 7 minutes.
Once thoroughly cooked, the internal temperature should reach 145ºF (63ºC). Serve
Nutritional Values (per serving): Calories: 181 Fat: 9g Carbs: 10g Protein: 22g

Salmon with Cauliflower

Prep time: 10 mins   Cook time: 25 mins
Serves 4
Ingredients
1 tablespoon coconut oil, melted
1 teaspoon ground turmeric
¼ cup coconut cream
1 pound (454 g) salmon fillet, diced
1 cup cauliflower, shredded
1 tablespoon dried cilantro

Directions
Combine salmon with cauliflower, dried cilantro, ground turmeric, coconut cream, and coconut oil.
Put the salmon mixture in the air fryer and cook it at 350ºF (177ºC) for 25 mins. Remember to stir the meal every 5 mins to prevent it from burning.
Nutritional Values (per serving): Calories: 250 Fat: 12g Carbs: 15g Protein: 20g

Baked Monkfish

Prep time: 20 mins   Cook time: 12 mins
Serves 2
Ingredients
2 tablespoons lime juice
Coarse salt and ground black pepper, to taste
1 teaspoon cayenne pepper
1 teaspoon dried thyme
½ teaspoon dried marjoram
½ teaspoon dried rosemary
2 teaspoons olive oil
1 cup celery, sliced
2 bell peppers, sliced
2 monkfish fillets
1 tablespoon coconut aminos
½ cup Kalamata olives, pitted and sliced

Directions
Heat olive oil in a nonstick skillet for 1 minute. Once it's hot, sauté the celery and peppers until they become tender, which should take around 4 minutes. Sprinkle with thyme, marjoram, and rosemary, then set aside.
Coat the fish fillets with coconut aminos, lime juice, salt, black pepper, and cayenne pepper. Place the fish fillets in the lightly greased air fryer basket and cook at 390ºF (199ºC) for 8 minutes.
Flip the fillets, add the olives, and continue cooking for an additional 4 minutes. Serve alongside the sautéed vegetables. Enjoy your meal!
Nutritional Values (per serving): Calories: 232 Fat: 10g Carbs: 10g Protein: 25g

Baked Salmon with Tomatoes and Olives

Prep time: 5 mins   **Cook time: 8 mins**
Serves 4
Ingredients
¼ teaspoon cayenne
¼ cup sliced Kalamata olives
4 lemon slices
1 teaspoon chopped fresh dill
2 Roma tomatoes, diced
2 tablespoons olive oil
4 (1½-inch-thick) salmon fillets
½ teaspoon salt

Directions
Heat up the air fryer to 380°F (193ºC).
Coat both sides of the salmon fillets with olive oil, then lightly season them with salt, cayenne, and dill.
Arrange the fillets in a single layer in the air fryer basket, then add a layer of tomatoes and olives on top. Place a lemon slice on each fillet.
Air fry for 8 minutes or until the salmon's internal temperature reaches 145°F (63ºC).
Nutritional Values (per serving): Calories: 201 Fat: 10g Carbs: 5g Protein: 20g

Garlicky Cod Fillets

Prep time: 10 mins Cook time: 10 to 12 mins
Serves 4
Ingredients
¼ teaspoon ground black pepper, or more to taste
1 teaspoon cayenne pepper
4 garlic cloves, minced
1 teaspoon dried basil
½ teaspoon dried oregano
1 teaspoon olive oil
4 cod fillets
¼ teaspoon fine sea salt
½ cup fresh Italian parsley, coarsely chopped
½ cup nondairy milk
1 Italian pepper, chopped

Directions
Gently apply olive oil to the sides and bottom of a baking dish. Keep it aside.
In a clean bowl, sprinkle the fillets with salt, black pepper, and cayenne pepper.
Using a food processor, blend the remaining ingredients until you have a smooth purée.
Combine the purée with the fillets in the bowl, ensuring they are evenly coated, and then transfer the mixture to the prepared baking dish.
Preheat the air fryer to 380ºF (193ºC).
Place the baking dish into the air fryer basket and bake for 10 to 12 minutes, or until the fish easily flakes when pressed with a fork.
Take it out of the basket and serve warm.
Nutritional Values (per serving): Calories: 187 Fat: 8g Carbs: 10g Protein: 20g

Baked Grouper with Tomatoes and Garlic

Prep time: 5 mins   **Cook time: 12 mins**
Serves 4
Ingredients
1 tomato, sliced
Juice of 1 lemon
¼ cup olive oil
¼ cup sliced Kalamata olives
¼ cup fresh dill, roughly chopped
4 grouper fillets
½ teaspoon salt
3 garlic cloves, minced

Directions
Heat the air fryer to 380ºF (193ºC).
Season the grouper fillets with salt on all sides, then put them in the air fryer basket and layer with minced garlic, tomato slices, olives, and fresh dill.
Pour lemon juice and olive oil over the grouper, then air fry for 10 to 12 minutes, or until the internal temperature reaches 145°F (63ºC).
Nutritional Values (per serving): Calories: 245 Fat: 11g Carbs: 5g Protein: 25g

Tuna Casserole

Prep time: 15 mins   Cook time: 15 mins
Serves 4
Ingredients
2 stalks celery, finely chopped
½ teaspoon red pepper flakes
2 medium zucchini, spiralized
2 (5-ounce / 142-g) cans albacore tuna
½ cup heavy cream
½ cup vegetable broth
2 tablespoons salted butter
¼ cup diced white onion
¼ cup chopped white mushrooms
2 tablespoons full-fat mayonnaise
¼ teaspoon xanthan gum
1 ounce (28 g) pork rinds, finely ground

Directions
Melt butter in a large saucepan over medium heat. Sauté onion, mushrooms, and celery until they release their aroma, which should take about 3 to 5 minutes.
Combine heavy cream, vegetable broth, mayonnaise, and xanthan gum in the saucepan. Reduce the heat and continue cooking for an additional 3 minutes until the mixture starts thickening.
Add red pepper flakes, zucchini, and tuna to the mixture. Turn off the heat and stir until the zucchini noodles are well-coated.
Transfer the mixture into a circular baking dish. Sprinkle ground pork rinds on top and cover the dish with foil. Place it in the air fryer basket. Set the air fryer temperature to 370ºF (188ºC) and timer for 15 minutes.
With 3 minutes left, uncover the casserole to brown the top. Serve it while it's warm.
Nutritional Values (per serving): Calories: 300 Fat: 18g Carbs: 20g Protein: 20g

Coconut Cream Mackerel

Prep time: 10 mins Cook time: 6 mins
Serves 4
Ingredients
1 teaspoon cumin seeds
1 garlic clove, peeled, chopped
2 pounds (907 g) mackerel fillet
1 cup coconut cream
1 teaspoon ground coriander

Directions
Roughly dice the mackerel and season it with coconut cream, ground coriander, cumin seeds, and garlic. Place the fish in the air fryer and cook at 400ºF (204ºC) for 6 minutes.
Nutritional Values (per serving): Calories: 227 Fat: 16g Carbs: 4g Protein: 20g

Shrimp Curry

Prep time: 30 mins   Cook time: 10 mins
Serves 4
Ingredients
1 teaspoon salt
¼ to ½ teaspoon cayenne pepper
1 pound (454 g) raw shrimp (21 to 25 count), peeled and deveined
1 tablespoon minced fresh ginger
1 tablespoon minced garlic
¾ cup unsweetened full-fat coconut milk
¼ cup finely chopped yellow onion
2 teaspoons garam masala
1 teaspoon ground turmeric
2 teaspoons chopped fresh cilantro

Directions
Combine coconut milk, onion, garam masala, ginger, garlic, turmeric, salt, and cayenne in a large bowl, ensuring they are thoroughly mixed.
Add the shrimp to the bowl and coat them with the sauce on all sides. Allow them to marinate at room temperature for 30 minutes.
Place the marinated shrimp and sauce in a baking pan and put the pan in the air fryer basket. Set the air fryer to 375ºF (191ºC) for 10 minutes, remembering to stir halfway through the cooking time. Transfer the cooked shrimp to a serving bowl or platter. Sprinkle cilantro over them and serve.
Nutritional Values (per serving): Calories: 200 Fat: 12g Carbs: 10g Protein: 25g

White Fish with Cauliflower

Prep time: 30 mins   Cook time: 13 mins
Serves 4
Ingredients
½ tablespoon cilantro, minced
2 ½ cups cooked white fish
Salt and freshly cracked black pepper, to taste
2 tablespoons sour cream
½ pound (227 g) cauliflower florets
½ teaspoon English mustard
2 tablespoons butter, room temperature

Directions
Cook the cauliflower until it's tender, then blend it until smooth. Transfer the cauliflower purée to a mixing bowl.
Combine the fish, cilantro, salt, and black pepper with the cauliflower purée.
Add sour cream, English mustard, and butter; mix until thoroughly combined. Shape the mixture into patties using your hands.
Refrigerate the patties for approximately 2 hours. Cook them at 395ºF (202ºC) for 13 minutes. Serve with extra English mustard on the side.
Nutritional Values (per serving): Calories: 226 Fat: 8g Carbs: 10g Protein: 25g

Smoky Shrimp and Chorizo Tapas

Prep time: 15 mins   Cook time: 10 mins
Serves 2 to 4
Ingredients
½ teaspoon smoked Spanish paprika
¼ teaspoon kosher salt
¼ teaspoon black pepper
1 tablespoon extra-virgin olive oil
1 small shallot, halved and thinly sliced
1 garlic clove, minced
4 ounces (113 g) Spanish (cured) chorizo, halved horizontally and sliced crosswise
½ pound (227 g) raw medium shrimp, peeled and deveined

1 tablespoon finely chopped fresh oregano
3 tablespoons fresh orange juice
1 tablespoon minced fresh parsley

Directions
Put the chorizo into a baking pan and place it in the air fryer basket. Set the air fryer to 375ºF (191ºC) for 5 minutes, or until the chorizo begins to brown and release its fat.
Meanwhile, in a clean bowl, mix the shrimp with olive oil, shallot, garlic, oregano, paprika, salt, and pepper. Ensure the shrimp is evenly coated.
Add the shrimp to the pan with the chorizo and stir to combine. Put the pan in the air fryer basket. Cook for 10 minutes, stirring halfway through the cooking time.
Transfer the cooked shrimp and chorizo to a serving dish. Drizzle with orange juice and toss to combine. Sprinkle with parsley.
Nutritional Values (per serving): Calories: 183 Fat: 9g Carbs: 10g Protein: 18g

Sweet Tilapia Fillets

Prep time: 5 mins   Cook time: 14 mins
Serves 4
Ingredients
4 tilapia fillets, boneless
1 teaspoon olive oil
2 tablespoons erythritol
1 tablespoon apple cider vinegar

Directions
Combine apple cider vinegar, olive oil, and erythritol in a mixture.
Rub the tilapia fillets with this sweet mixture and place them in a single layer in the air fryer basket. Cook the fish at 360ºF (182ºC) for 7 minutes on each side.
Nutritional Values (per serving): Calories: 144 Fat: 3g Carbs: 10g Protein: 20g

Parmesan Lobster Tails

Prep time: 5 mins   **Cook time: 7 mins**
Serves 4
Ingredients
¼ teaspoon salt
¼ cup grated Parmesan cheese
½ ounce (14 g) plain pork rinds, finely crushed
¼ teaspoon ground black pepper
4 (4-ounce / 113-g) lobster tails
2 tablespoons salted butter, melted
1½ teaspoons Cajun seasoning, divided

Directions
Gently cut open lobster tails using scissors and remove the meat from the shells, placing it on top of the shells.
Brush the lobster meat with butter and sprinkle 1 teaspoon of Cajun seasoning, ¼ teaspoon for each tail.
Combine the remaining Cajun seasoning, salt, pepper, Parmesan, and pork rinds in a small bowl. Gently press ¼ of this mixture onto the meat of each lobster tail.
Carefully place the tails into the air fryer basket without greasing it. Set the temperature to 400ºF (204ºC) and air fry for 7 minutes. The lobster tails will become crispy and golden on top and should have an internal temperature of at least 145ºF (63ºC) when done. Serve them while they're warm.
Nutritional Values (per serving): Calories: 229 Fat: 14g Carbs: 3g Protein: 20g

Calamari with Hot Sauce

Prep time: 10 mins   **Cook time: 6 mins**
Serves 2
Ingredients
2 tablespoons keto hot sauce
1 tablespoon avocado oil
10 ounces (283 g) calamari, trimmed

Directions
Cut the calamari into slices and drizzle them with avocado oil.

Place the calamari in the air fryer and cook at 400ºF (204ºC) for 3 minutes on each side.
Transfer the cooked calamari to a serving plate and sprinkle them with hot sauce.
Nutritional Values (per serving): Calories: 350 Fat: 17g Carbs: 9g Protein: 21g

Browned Shrimp Patties

Prep time: 15 mins   **Cook time: 10 to 12 mins**
Serves 4
Ingredients
¼ cup chopped red bell pepper
¼ cup chopped celery
½ pound (227 g) raw shrimp, shelled, deveined, and chopped finely
2 cups cooked sushi rice
¼ cup chopped green onion
½ teaspoon Old Bay seasoning
½ cup plain bread crumbs
2 teaspoons Worcestershire sauce
½ teaspoon salt
½ teaspoon garlic powder
Cooking spray

Directions
Preheat the air fryer to 390ºF (199ºC).
Combine all the ingredients in a large bowl, excluding the bread crumbs and oil, and mix them together.
Take scoops of the shrimp mixture and shape them into 8 evenly-sized patties, ensuring they are no thicker than ½-inch. Roll these patties in breadcrumbs placed on a plate and coat both sides with cooking spray.
Arrange the patties in the air fryer basket, possibly in batches to prevent overcrowding.
Air fry for 10 to 12 minutes, flipping the patties halfway through, or until they develop a crispy brown exterior.
Divide the patties among four plates and serve them while they're still warm.
Nutritional Values (per serving): Calories: 276 Fat: 19g Carbs: 4.4g Protein: 22g

Lemon Mahi-Mahi

Prep time: 5 mins   **Cook time: 14 mins**
Serves 2
Ingredients
1 tablespoon olive oil
1 tablespoon chopped fresh dill
2 lemon slices
¼ teaspoon salt
Oil, for spraying
2 (6-ounce / 170-g) mahi-mahi fillets
1 tablespoon lemon juice
¼ teaspoon freshly ground black pepper

Directions
Line the air fryer basket with parchment paper and lightly coat it with oil.
Arrange the mahi-mahi in the prepared basket. Combine the lemon juice and olive oil in a small bowl. Brush this mixture evenly over the mahi-mahi. Sprinkle the mahi-mahi with salt and black pepper, then garnish with dill.
Air fry at 400ºF (204ºC) for 12 to 14 minutes, adjusting the time based on the fillets' thickness until they flake easily.
Transfer the cooked fish to plates, place a lemon slice on each, and serve.
Nutritional Values (per serving): Calories: 238 Fat: 6g Carbs: 19g Protein: 33g

Tilapia Almondine

Prep time: 10 mins   **Cook time: 10 mins**
Serves 2
Ingredients
1 teaspoon black pepper
2 tilapia fillets
½ cup thinly sliced almonds
Vegetable oil spray
½ teaspoon kosher salt
¼ cup mayonnaise
½ cup almond flour or fine dried bread crumbs
2 tablespoons salted butter or ghee, melted

Directions
Combine almond flour, butter, pepper, and salt in a small bowl.

Coat both sides of each fish fillet with mayonnaise, then dip them into the almond flour mixture. Sprinkle sliced almonds on one side of each fillet and press gently to make them stick.
Lightly spray the air fryer basket with vegetable oil. Arrange the fish fillets in the basket. Set the air fryer to 325ºF (163ºC) for 10 minutes, or until the fish easily flakes with a fork.
Nutritional Values (per serving): Calories: 212 Fat: 7.6g Carbs: 13g Protein: 23g

Almond Pesto Salmon

Prep time: 5 mins   **Cook time: 12 mins**
Serves 2
Ingredients
2 (1½-inch-thick) salmon fillets (about 4 ounces / 113 g each)
2 tablespoons unsalted butter, melted
¼ cup pesto
¼ cup sliced almonds, roughly chopped

Directions
Combine pesto and almonds in a small bowl, then set it aside.
Put the fillets in a circular baking dish.
Brush each fillet with butter and evenly spread half of the pesto mixture on top of each fillet.
Place the dish in the air fryer basket.
Set the air fryer temperature to 390ºF (199ºC) and timer for 12 minutes.
The salmon will easily flake when fully cooked, and it should reach an internal temperature of at least 145ºF (63ºC). Serve while warm.
Nutritional Values (per serving): Calories: 520 Fat: 39g Carbs: 13g Protein: 30g

Scallops in Lemon-Butter Sauce

Prep time: 10 mins   Cook time: 6 mins
Serves 2
Ingredients
2 teaspoons capers, drained and chopped
1 teaspoon grated lemon zest
1 clove garlic, minced
2 tablespoons unsalted butter, melted
2 tablespoons chopped flat-leaf parsley
1 tablespoon fresh lemon juice
8 large dry sea scallops (about ¾ pound/340 g)
Salt and freshly ground black pepper, to taste
2 tablespoons olive oil

Directions
Preheat the air fryer to 400ºF (204ºC). Pat the scallops dry using a paper towel and lightly season them with salt and pepper. Brush the scallops with olive oil and arrange them in a single layer in the air fryer basket. Remember to pause halfway through cooking to flip the scallops. Air fry for approximately 6 minutes until they become firm and opaque.
While the scallops are cooking, combine oil, butter, parsley, lemon juice, capers, lemon zest, and garlic in a small bowl. Drizzle this mixture over the scallops just before serving.
Nutritional Values (per serving): Calories: 207 Fat: 10g Carbs: 7g Protein: 24g

Pesto Shrimp with Wild Rice Pilaf

Prep time: 5 mins   Cook time: 5 mins
Serves 4
Ingredients
1 lemon, sliced
2 cups cooked wild rice pilaf
1 pound (454 g) medium shrimp, peeled and deveined
¼ cup pesto sauce

Directions

Preheat the air fryer to 360°F (182ºC).
In a medium-sized bowl, coat the shrimp thoroughly with the pesto sauce.
Arrange the shrimp in a single layer in the air fryer basket. Lay the lemon slices on top of the shrimp and air fry for 5 minutes.
Take out the lemon slices and discard them. Serve a quarter of the shrimp over ½ cup of wild rice, accompanied by your favorite steamed vegetables.
Nutritional Values (per serving): Calories: 567 Fat: 28g Carbs: 43g Protein: 27g

Fish Taco Bowl

Prep time: 10 mins   Cook time: 12 mins
Serves 4
Ingredients
$^1/_3$ cup mayonnaise
¼ teaspoon ground black pepper
4 (4-ounce / 113-g) cod fillets
4 cups finely shredded green cabbage
½ teaspoon salt
¼ teaspoon garlic powder
¼ teaspoon ground cumin
¼ cup chopped pickled jalapeños

Directions
Season cod with salt, garlic powder, and cumin, then put it in the air fryer basket without greasing it. Set the air fryer temperature to 350ºF (177ºC) and air fry for 12 minutes, flipping the fillets halfway through cooking. The cod should easily flake and have an internal temperature of at least 145ºF (63ºC) when done.
In a large bowl, mix cabbage with mayonnaise, pepper, and jalapeños until everything is well-coated. Serve the warm cod over the cabbage slaw on four medium plates.
Nutritional Values (per serving): Calories: 412 Fat: 13g Carbs: 40g Protein: 30g

Garlic Butter Shrimp Scampi

Prep time: 5 mins   **Cook time: 8 mins**
Serves 4
Ingredients
Sauce:
2 tablespoons chopped fresh basil leaves
1 tablespoon lemon juice
1 tablespoon chopped fresh parsley, plus more for garnish
¼ cup unsalted butter
2 tablespoons fish stock or chicken broth
2 cloves garlic, minced
1 teaspoon red pepper flakes
Shrimp:
Fresh basil sprigs, for garnish
1 pound (454 g) large shrimp, peeled and deveined, tails removed
Directions
Heat up the air fryer to 350ºF (177ºC).
Place all the sauce ingredients in a baking pan and mix them together.
Transfer the baking pan to the air fryer and air fry for 3 minutes, or until the sauce is heated through.
Once the sauce is ready, add the shrimp to the baking pan, ensuring they are coated in the sauce.
Return the pan to the air fryer and cook for an additional 5 minutes, or until the shrimp turn pink and opaque. Stir the shrimp twice during the cooking process. Serve the dish garnished with parsley and basil sprigs.
Nutritional Values (per serving): Calories: 680 Fat: 33g Carbs: 51g Protein: 32g

Tuna Patty Sliders

Prep time: 15 mins Cook time: 10 to 15 mins
Serves 4
Ingredients
1 tablespoon sriracha
¾ teaspoon black pepper
10 whole-wheat slider buns
3 (5-ounce / 142-g) cans tuna, packed in water
$^2/_3$ cup whole-wheat panko bread crumbs
$^1/_3$ cup shredded Parmesan cheese

Cooking spray
Directions
Preheat the air fryer to 350ºF (177ºC).
Lightly spray the air fryer basket with cooking spray.
In a medium bowl, mix together tuna, bread crumbs, Parmesan cheese, sriracha, and black pepper until well combined. Shape the mixture into 10 patties. Place the patties in the air fryer basket in a single layer. Give them a light spray with cooking spray. You may need to cook them in batches.
Air fry for 6 to 8 minutes, then flip the patties over, and lightly spray them again with cooking spray. Continue air frying until they are golden brown and crisp, for an additional 4 to 7 minutes. Serve the patties while they're warm.
Nutritional Values (per serving): Calories: 125 Fat: 6.5g Carbs: 7g Protein: 10g

Snapper with Fruit

Prep time: 15 mins   Cook time: 9 to 13 mins
Serves 4
Ingredients
1 tablespoon freshly squeezed lemon juice
1 tablespoon honey
½ teaspoon dried thyme
3 plums, halved and pitted
1 cup red grapes
4 (4-ounce / 113-g) red snapper fillets
2 teaspoons olive oil
3 nectarines, halved and pitted

Directions
Place the red snapper in the air fryer basket and drizzle it with olive oil. Air fry at 390ºF (199ºC) for 4 minutes.
Remove the basket and add the nectarines and plums. Scatter the grapes over everything.
Drizzle lemon juice and honey over the fruit and sprinkle with thyme.
Return the basket to the air fryer and air fry for an additional 5 to 9 minutes, or until the fish flakes easily when tested with a fork and the fruit becomes tender. Serve right away.
Nutritional Values (per serving): Calories: 334 Fat: 22g Carbs: 5g Protein: 23g

Tuna Steaks with Olive Tapenade

Prep time: 10 mins   Cook time: 10 mins
Serves 4
Ingredients
½ lemon, sliced into 4 wedges
4 (6-ounce / 170-g) ahi tuna steaks
1 tablespoon olive oil
Salt and freshly ground black pepper, to taste
Olive Tapenade:
1 tablespoon chopped fresh parsley
1 clove garlic
½ cup pitted kalamata olives
1 tablespoon olive oil
2 teaspoons red wine vinegar
1 teaspoon capers, drained
Directions
Preheat the air fryer to 400ºF (204ºC).
Sprinkle the tuna steaks with olive oil and season them with salt and black pepper. Place the tuna steaks in a single layer in the air fryer basket. Remember to flip the steaks halfway through the cooking time. Air fry for 10 minutes until the fish is firm.
To prepare the tapenade: In a food processor equipped with a metal blade, combine olives, olive oil, parsley, garlic, vinegar, and capers. Pulse until the mixture is finely chopped, pausing to scrape down the sides of the bowl if necessary. Spoon the tapenade over the tuna steaks and serve with lemon wedges.
Nutritional Values (per serving): Calories: 263 Fat: 10g Carbs: 3g Protein: 35g

Golden Shrimp

Prep time: 20 mins   Cook time: 7 mins
Serves 4
Ingredients
½ teaspoon celery seeds
½ teaspoon porcini powder
2 egg whites
½ cup coconut flour
1 cup Parmigiano-Reggiano, grated
½ teaspoon onion powder

½ teaspoon ground black pepper
1½ pounds (680 g) shrimp, deveined
1 teaspoon garlic powder
½ teaspoon dried rosemary
½ teaspoon sea salt
Directions
Combine the egg with coconut flour and Parmigiano-Reggiano. Add seasonings and mix thoroughly. Dip your shrimp into the batter, ensuring they are fully coated on all sides.
Cook the shrimp in the preheated air fryer at 390ºF (199ºC) for 5 to 7 minutes or until they turn golden brown. Work in batches if necessary. Serve with lemon wedges if desired.
Nutritional Values (per serving): Calories: 210 Fat: 9g Carbs: 23g Protein: 9g

Firecracker Shrimp

Prep time: 10 mins   Cook time: 7 mins
Serves 4
Ingredients
¼ cup full-fat mayonnaise
⅛ teaspoon ground black pepper
½ teaspoon Old Bay seasoning
¼ teaspoon garlic powder
1 pound (454 g) medium shelled and deveined shrimp
2 tablespoons salted butter, melted
2 tablespoons sriracha
¼ teaspoon powdered erythritol

Directions
In a clean bowl, coat the shrimp with butter, Old Bay seasoning, and garlic powder. Then, place the shrimp into the air fryer basket.
Set the air fryer temperature to 400ºF (204ºC) and timer for 7 minutes.
Flip the shrimp halfway through the cooking time; they should turn bright pink when fully cooked.
In another clean bowl, combine sriracha, powdered erythritol, mayonnaise, and pepper. Toss the cooked shrimp in this spicy mixture and serve immediately.
Nutritional Values (per serving): Calories: 600 Fat: 39g Carbs: 21g Protein: 36g

Tuna Avocado Bites

Prep time: 10 mins   **Cook time: 7 mins**
Makes 12 bites
Ingredients
1 medium avocado, peeled, pitted, and mashed
½ cup blanched finely ground almond flour, divided
2 teaspoons coconut oil
1 (10-ounce / 283-g) can tuna, drained
¼ cup full-fat mayonnaise
1 stalk celery, chopped
Directions
Combine tuna, mayonnaise, celery, and mashed avocado in a large bowl. Shape the mixture into balls.
Roll the balls in almond flour and lightly spray them with coconut oil. Place the balls into the air fryer basket.
Set the air fryer temperature to 400ºF (204ºC) and the timer for 7 minutes.
After 5 minutes, gently flip the tuna bites. Serve them while they're warm.
Nutritional Values (per serving): Calories: 185 Fat: 16g Carbs: 6g Protein: 11g

Cajun Catfish Cakes with Cheese

Prep time: 5 mins   **Cook time: 35 mins**
Serves 4
Ingredients
1 cup shredded Swiss cheese
1 teaspoon baking soda
1 teaspoon Cajun seasoning
½ cup buttermilk
2 catfish fillets
3 ounces (85 g) butter
1 cup shredded Parmesan cheese
1 teaspoon baking powder
Directions
Boil a pot of salted water. Place the catfish fillets in the boiling water and allow them to boil for 5 minutes until they turn opaque.
Remove the fillets from the pot and transfer them to a mixing bowl.

Use a fork to flake the fillets into small pieces. Add the remaining ingredients to the bowl with the fish and mix until well combined. Divide the fish mixture into 12 equal portions and shape each portion into a patty. Preheat the air fryer to 380ºF (193ºC). Arrange the patties in the air fryer basket and air fry them in batches for 15 minutes until they turn golden brown and are thoroughly cooked. Flip the patties halfway through the cooking time.
Allow the patties to rest for 5 minutes before serving.
Nutritional Values (per serving): Calories: 467 Fat: 37g Carbs: 5g Protein: 12g

Country Shrimp

Prep time: 10 mins Cook time: 15 to 20 mins
Serves 4
Ingredients
1 tablespoon Old Bay seasoning
2 tablespoons olive oil
2 corn cobs, quartered
1 zucchini, cut into bite-sized pieces
1 red bell pepper, cut into chunks
1 pound (454 g) large shrimp, deveined, with tails on
1 pound (454 g) smoked turkey sausage, cut into thick slices
Cooking spray

Directions
Preheat the air fryer to 400ºF (204ºC) and lightly spray the air fryer basket with cooking spray.
In a large bowl, combine the shrimp, turkey sausage, corn, zucchini, bell pepper, and Old Bay seasoning. Toss to coat all the ingredients with the spices. Then, add the olive oil and toss again until everything is evenly coated.
Spread this mixture in the air fryer basket in a single layer, remembering to cook in batches if necessary.
Air fry for 15 to 20 minutes, or until everything is thoroughly cooked, shaking the basket every 5 minutes for even cooking. Serve immediately.
Nutritional Values (per serving): Calories: 187 Fat: 9g Carbs: 12g Protein: 10g

Shrimp Bake

Prep time: 15 mins   Cook time: 5 mins
Serves 4
Ingredients
1 cup Cheddar cheese, shredded
½ teaspoon coconut oil
1 teaspoon ground coriander
14 ounces (397 g) shrimp, peeled
1 egg, beaten
½ cup coconut milk

Directions
Combine shrimp with egg, coconut milk, Cheddar cheese, coconut oil, and ground coriander in a mixing bowl.
Transfer the mixture into baking ramekins and place them in the air fryer.
Cook the shrimp at 400ºF (204ºC) for 5 minutes.
Nutritional Values (per serving): Calories: 170 Fat: 7g Carbs: 3g Protein: 22g

Pecan-Crusted Catfish

Prep time: 5 mins   Cook time: 12 mins
Serves 4
Ingredients
½ cup pecan meal
1 teaspoon fine sea salt
¼ teaspoon ground black pepper
4 (4-ounce / 113-g) catfish fillets
Avocado oil for spraying
For Garnish (Optional):
Fresh oregano
Pecan halves

Directions
Lightly spraying the air fryer basket with avocado oil. Preheat the air fryer to 375ºF (191ºC).

In a clean bowl, combine pecan meal, salt, and pepper. One by one, coat the catfish fillets thoroughly in this mixture, pressing the pecan meal onto the fillets using your hands. Spray the coated fish with avocado oil and place them in the air fryer basket.
Air fry the catfish for 12 minutes, or until it flakes easily and is no longer translucent in the center, flipping them halfway through the cooking time.
Optionally, garnish with oregano sprigs and pecan halves before serving.

Nutritional Values (per serving): Calories: 341 Fat: 22g Carbs: 4g Protein: 23g

CHAPTER 5
CHICKEN RECIPES

Crispy Air Fried Chicken Wings

**Prep Time: 15 mins Cooking Time: 25 mins
Servings: 4**
Ingredients:
1 pound chicken wings
1 tablespoon olive oil
1/2 teaspoon salt
1/2 teaspoon black pepper
1/2 teaspoon paprika
1/2 teaspoon garlic powder
1/2 teaspoon onion powder
Cooking spray
Directions:
Preheat your air fryer to 375°F (190°C).
In a large bowl, toss the chicken wings with olive oil, salt, black pepper, paprika, garlic powder, and onion powder until well coated.
Place the seasoned wings in the air fryer basket in a single layer, making sure they are not overcrowded.
Spray the wings lightly with cooking spray to help them get crispy.
Air fry the wings for 12-15 mins, then flip them over and air fry for an additional 10-12 mins, or until they are golden brown and cooked through (reaching an internal temperature of 165°F or 74°C).
Remove the wings from the air fryer and let them rest for a few mins before serving.
Nutritional Values (per serving): Calories: 223 kcal Protein: 19g Carbohydrates: 0.5g Fat: 15g Fiber: 0.1g

Lemon Herb Roast Chicken

**Prep Time: 20 mins Cooking Time: 40 mins
Servings: 4**
Ingredients:
1 whole chicken (about 4 pounds)
2 tablespoons olive oil
2 lemons, halved
4 cloves garlic, minced
1 teaspoon dried thyme
1 teaspoon dried rosemary
1 teaspoon dried sage
Salt and black pepper to taste
Directions:
Preheat your air fryer to 350°F (175°C).

Rinse the chicken inside and out, then pat it dry with paper towels. Rub the chicken all over with olive oil, inside and out.
Season the chicken cavity with salt, pepper, and half of the minced garlic.
Place the lemon halves inside the chicken's cavity.
In a small bowl, mix together the dried thyme, rosemary, sage, remaining minced garlic, salt, and pepper. Rub the herb mixture all over the chicken's skin. Place the seasoned chicken in the air fryer basket, breast-side down.
Air fry for 20 mins, then carefully flip the chicken breast-side up.
Continue to air fry for another 20-25 mins or until the chicken's internal temperature reaches 165°F (74°C).
Let the it rest for a few mins before serving.
Nutritional Values (per serving): Calories: 350 kcal Protein: 26g Carbohydrates: 4g Fat: 26g Fiber: 2g

BBQ Chicken Drumsticks

**Prep Time: 15 mins Cooking Time: 25 mins
Servings: 4**
Ingredients:
8 chicken drumsticks
1/2 cup BBQ sauce (your favorite brand)
1 teaspoon olive oil
1/2 teaspoon garlic powder
1/2 teaspoon onion powder
1/2 teaspoon paprika
Salt and black pepper to taste
Directions:
Preheat your air fryer to 375°F (190°C).
In a bowl, mix the BBQ sauce, olive oil, garlic powder, onion powder, paprika, salt, and black pepper.
Coat the chicken drumsticks evenly with the BBQ sauce mixture.
Place the drumsticks in the air fryer basket in a single layer.
Air fry for 12-15 mins, then flip the drumsticks and air fry for an additional 10-12 mins, or until they are cooked through and the skin is crispy.
Check for doneness (internal temperature should be 165°F or 74°C).
Serve with extra BBQ sauce on the side for dipping.
Nutritional Values (per serving): Calories: 280 kcal Protein: 26g Carbohydrates: 13g Fat: 13g Fiber: 0.5g

Garlic Parmesan Chicken Tenders

Prep Time: 15 mins Cooking Time: 15 mins
Servings: 4
Ingredients:
1 pound chicken tenders
1 cup breadcrumbs
1/2 cup grated Parmesan cheese
2 teaspoons garlic powder
1 teaspoon dried parsley
Salt and black pepper to taste
2 large eggs, beaten

Directions:
Preheat your air fryer to 375°F (190°C).
In a bowl, combine breadcrumbs, grated Parmesan cheese, garlic powder, dried parsley, salt, and black pepper.
Dip each chicken tender into the beaten eggs, allowing excess to drip off, and then coat them with the breadcrumb mixture, pressing the breadcrumbs onto the chicken to adhere.
Place the coated chicken tenders in the air fryer basket in a single layer.
Air fry for 10-12 mins, flipping them halfway through, or until the chicken tenders are golden brown and cooked through (internal temperature of 165°F or 74°C).
Serve with your favorite dipping sauce.
Nutritional Values (per serving): Calories: 322 kcal Protein: 32g Carbohydrates: 19g Fat: 12g Fiber: 1g

Spicy Buffalo Chicken Bites

Prep Time: 15 mins Cooking Time: 15 mins
Servings: 4
Ingredients:
1 pound boneless, skinless chicken breast, cut into bite-sized pieces
1/2 cup hot sauce (your preferred brand)
2 tablespoons unsalted butter, melted
1 teaspoon garlic powder
1/2 teaspoon onion powder
1/2 teaspoon paprika
Salt and black pepper to taste
Blue cheese dressing and celery sticks for serving (optional)
Directions:
Preheat your air fryer to 375°F (190°C).

In a bowl, mix the hot sauce, melted butter, garlic powder, onion powder, paprika, salt, and black pepper.
Toss the chicken pieces in the buffalo sauce mixture until they are well coated.
Place the coated chicken bites in the air fryer basket in a single layer.
Air fry for 12-15 mins, shaking the basket or flipping the chicken pieces halfway through, until they are crispy and cooked through.
Check for doneness (internal temperature should be 165°F or 74°C).
Serve with blue cheese dressing and celery sticks for a classic pairing.
Nutritional Values (per serving): Calories: 257 kcal Protein: 25g Carbohydrates: 3g Fat: 15g Fiber: 0.5g

Teriyaki Chicken Skewers

Prep Time: 20 mins Cooking Time: 15 mins
Servings: 4
Ingredients:
1 pound boneless, skinless chicken thighs, cut into 1-inch pieces
1/2 cup teriyaki sauce (store-bought or homemade)
2 tablespoons soy sauce
2 cloves garlic, minced
1 teaspoon fresh ginger, grated
1/2 teaspoon sesame seeds (optional)
Bamboo skewers, soaked in water for 30 mins

Directions:
Preheat your air fryer to 375°F (190°C).
In a bowl, combine teriyaki sauce, soy sauce, minced garlic, and grated ginger to make the marinade.
Thread the chicken pieces onto the soaked bamboo skewers.
Place the chicken skewers in a shallow dish and pour the marinade over them. Allow them to marinate for 15 mins, turning occasionally.
Arrange the chicken skewers in the air fryer basket, making sure they are not overcrowded.
Air fry for 10-12 mins, turning them halfway through, until the chicken is cooked through.
If desired, sprinkle with sesame seeds before serving.
Nutritional Values (per serving): Calories: 224 kcal Protein: 25g Carbohydrates: 13g Fat: 7g Fiber: 0.5g

Honey Mustard Glazed Chicken Thighs

Prep Time: 15 mins Cooking Time: 20 mins
Servings: 4
Ingredients:
4 bone-in, skin-on chicken thighs
1/4 cup honey
2 tablespoons Dijon mustard
2 cloves garlic, minced
1 tablespoon olive oil
1/2 teaspoon dried thyme
Salt and black pepper to taste
Directions:
Preheat your air fryer to 375°F (190°C).
In a bowl, whisk together honey, Dijon mustard, minced garlic, olive oil, dried thyme, salt, and black pepper.
Place the chicken thighs in a resealable plastic bag and pour the honey mustard mixture over them. Seal the bag and massage the marinade into the chicken. Marinate for 10-15 mins.
Remove the chicken from the marinade and place them in the air fryer basket, skin-side up.
Air fry for 18-20 mins, until the chicken thighs are cooked through and the skin is crispy.
Check for doneness (internal temperature should be 165°F or 74°C).
Serve the chicken thighs with any remaining honey mustard glaze drizzled over the top.
Nutritional Values (per serving): Calories: 329 kcal Protein: 21g Carbohydrates: 18g Fat: 18g Fiber: 0.5g

Paprika-Rubbed Air Fryer Chicken

Prep Time: 15 mins Cooking Time: 25 mins
Servings: 4
Ingredients:
4 bone-in, skin-on chicken thighs
2 teaspoons paprika
1 teaspoon garlic powder
1 teaspoon onion powder
1/2 teaspoon dried thyme
1/2 teaspoon dried oregano
Salt and black pepper to taste
1 tablespoon olive oil

Directions:
Preheat your air fryer to 375°F (190°C).
In a small bowl, combine paprika, garlic powder, onion powder, dried thyme, dried oregano, salt, and black pepper.
Rub the chicken thighs with olive oil and then generously coat them with the paprika spice mixture, ensuring they are well covered.
Place the chicken thighs in the air fryer basket, skin-side up.
Air fry for 20-25 mins, until the chicken is cooked through and the skin is crispy.
Check for doneness (internal temperature should be 165°F or 74°C).
Serve hot, garnished with fresh herbs if desired.
Nutritional Values (per serving): Calories: 288 kcal Protein: 22g Carbohydrates: 10g Fat: 20g Fiber: 0.5g

Herbed Cornish Hens

Prep Time: 20 mins Cooking Time: 30 mins Servings: 2
Ingredients:
2 Cornish hens, halved
2 tablespoons olive oil
1 teaspoon dried thyme
1 teaspoon dried rosemary
1 teaspoon dried sage
Salt and black pepper to taste
2 cloves garlic, minced

Directions:
Preheat your air fryer to 375°F (190°C).
In a small bowl, mix together the dried thyme, dried rosemary, dried sage, minced garlic, salt, and black pepper.
Rub each Cornish hen half with olive oil and then season them with the herb mixture, making sure to coat them evenly.
Place the Cornish hen halves in the air fryer basket.
Air fry for 25-30 mins, flipping them halfway through the cooking time, until they are golden brown and cooked through.
Check for doneness (internal temperature should be 165°F or 74°C).
Let the Cornish hens rest for a few mins before serving.
Nutritional Values (per serving): Calories: 451 kcal Protein: 45g Carbohydrates: 7g Fat: 30g Fiber: 0.1g

Panko-Crusted Chicken Cutlets

Prep Time: 15 mins Cooking Time: 12 mins
Servings: 4
Ingredients:
4 boneless, skinless chicken breasts, pounded to 1/2-inch thickness
1 cup panko breadcrumbs
1/2 cup grated Parmesan cheese
1 teaspoon garlic powder
1 teaspoon onion powder
1/2 teaspoon dried basil
Salt and black pepper to taste
2 large eggs, beaten
Cooking spray
Directions:
Preheat your air fryer to 375°F (190°C).
In a shallow dish, combine panko breadcrumbs, grated Parmesan cheese, garlic powder, onion powder, dried basil, salt, and black pepper.
Dip each chicken breast into the beaten eggs, allowing excess to drip off, and then coat them with the breadcrumb mixture, pressing the breadcrumbs onto the chicken to adhere.
Place the coated chicken cutlets in the air fryer basket in a single layer.
Lightly spray the chicken cutlets with cooking spray to help them crisp up.
Air fry for 6 mins, then flip the chicken cutlets and air fry for an additional 6 mins or until they are golden brown and cooked through.
Check for doneness (internal temperature should be 165°F or 74°C). Serve with your favorite dipping sauce or over a salad.
Nutritional Values (per serving): Calories: 312 kcal Protein: 35g Carbohydrates: 12g Fat: 15g Fiber: 1g

Cajun Blackened Turkey Breast

Prep Time: 15 mins Cooking Time: 15 mins
Servings: 4
Ingredients:
4 turkey breast fillets
2 tablespoons olive oil
2 tablespoons Cajun seasoning
1 teaspoon paprika
1/2 teaspoon garlic powder
1/2 teaspoon onion powder
Salt and black pepper to taste
Cooking spray
Directions:
Preheat your air fryer to 375°F (190°C).

In a small bowl, combine Cajun seasoning, paprika, garlic powder, onion powder, salt, and black pepper. Brush each turkey breast fillet with olive oil and then evenly coat them with the Cajun spice mixture, pressing the spices onto the turkey.
Place the seasoned turkey fillets in the air fryer basket. Lightly spray the turkey with cooking spray to enhance crispiness.
Air fry for 7-8 mins, flip the turkey fillets, and air fry for another 7-8 mins or until they are cooked through and have a blackened appearance.
Check for doneness (internal temperature should be 165°F or 74°C). Serve with your choice of side dishes.
Nutritional Values (per serving): Calories: 254 kcal Protein: 35g Carbohydrates: 9g Fat: 11g Fiber: 1g

Mediterranean Stuffed Chicken Breast

Prep Time: 20 mins Cooking Time: 25 mins
Servings: 4
Ingredients:
4 boneless, skinless chicken breasts
1 cup spinach leaves, chopped
1/2 cup roasted red peppers, chopped
1/4 cup crumbled feta cheese
2 cloves garlic, minced
1 teaspoon dried oregano
Salt and black pepper to taste
1 tablespoon olive oil
Directions:
Preheat your air fryer to 375°F (190°C).
In a bowl, combine chopped spinach, roasted red peppers, crumbled feta cheese, minced garlic, dried oregano, salt, and black pepper to create the stuffing mixture.
Carefully cut a pocket into each chicken breast.
Stuff each chicken breast with the Mediterranean mixture, dividing it evenly among them.
Secure the openings with toothpicks to keep the filling in place.
Brush each stuffed chicken breast with olive oil and season with additional salt and black pepper, if desired.
Place the stuffed chicken breasts in the air fryer basket.
Air fry for 20-25 mins, turning them halfway through, until the chicken is cooked through.
Check for doneness (internal temperature should be 165°F or 74°C). Remove the toothpicks before serving.
Nutritional Values (per serving): Calories: 276 kcal Protein: 36g Carbohydrates: 5g Fat: 12g Fiber: 2g

Asian Sesame Chicken

Prep Time: 15 mins Cooking Time: 15 mins
Servings: 4
Ingredients:
1 pound boneless, skinless chicken breasts, cut into bite-sized pieces
1/4 cup soy sauce
2 tablespoons honey
1 tablespoon rice vinegar
1 tablespoon sesame oil
2 cloves garlic, minced
1 teaspoon fresh ginger, grated
1 tablespoon sesame seeds (for garnish)
Green onions, chopped (for garnish)
Cooked rice or steamed broccoli (for serving)
Directions:
Preheat your air fryer to 375°F (190°C).
In a bowl, whisk together soy sauce, honey, rice vinegar, sesame oil, minced garlic, and grated ginger to create the sauce.
Place the chicken pieces in the sauce and let them marinate for 10-15 mins.
Remove the chicken from the marinade and place them in the air fryer basket in a single layer.
Air fry for 10-12 mins, shaking the basket or flipping the chicken pieces halfway through, until they are cooked through.
Check for doneness (internal temperature should be 165°F or 74°C).
Serve the Asian sesame chicken garnished with sesame seeds and chopped green onions. You can serve it over cooked rice or with steamed broccoli if desired.
Nutritional Values (per serving, without optional sides): Calories: 243 kcal Protein: 25g Carbohydrates: 11g Fat: 7g Fiber: 0.5g

Coconut Curry Chicken

Prep Time: 20 mins Cooking Time: 20 mins
Servings: 4
Ingredients:
1 pound boneless, skinless chicken thighs, cut into chunks
1 can (14 ounces) coconut milk
2 tablespoons red curry paste
1 tablespoon fish sauce
1 tablespoon brown sugar
1 red bell pepper, sliced
1 onion, sliced
1 tablespoon vegetable oil
Fresh cilantro leaves (for garnish)
Cooked rice (for serving)
Directions:
Preheat your air fryer to 375°F (190°C).
In a bowl, whisk together coconut milk, red curry paste, fish sauce, and brown sugar to create the curry sauce.
Heat the vegetable oil in a skillet over medium heat. Add the sliced bell pepper and onion and sauté until they begin to soften.
Add the chicken chunks to the skillet and cook until they are no longer pink.
Pour the curry sauce over the chicken and vegetables, stirring to combine. Transfer the chicken curry mixture to the air fryer basket.
Air fry for 15-20 mins, stirring once or twice, until the chicken is cooked through and the sauce has thickened.
Serve the coconut curry chicken over cooked rice and garnish with fresh cilantro leaves.
Nutritional Values (per serving, without rice): Calories: 333 kcal Protein: 20g Carbohydrates: 11g Fat: 24g Fiber: 2g

Rosemary Lemon Cornish Game Hens

Prep Time: 20 mins Cooking Time: 35 mins
Servings: 2
Ingredients:
2 Cornish game hens
2 tablespoons olive oil
2 teaspoons fresh rosemary, minced
2 cloves garlic, minced
Zest and juice of 1 lemon
Salt and black pepper to taste
Directions:
Preheat your air fryer to 375°F (190°C).
In a bowl, combine olive oil, minced rosemary, minced garlic, lemon zest, lemon juice, salt, and black pepper to create the marinade.
Rinse the Cornish game hens inside and out, then pat them dry with paper towels.
Rub the marinade all over the hens, both on the skin and inside the cavity. Place the hens in the air fryer basket.
Air fry for 30-35 mins, turning them halfway through, until the hens are golden brown and cooked through.
Check for doneness (internal temperature should be 165°F or 74°C).
Allow the Cornish game hens to rest for a few mins before serving.
Nutritional Values (per serving): Calories: 403 kcal Protein: 35g Carbohydrates: 12g Fat: 28g Fiber: 0.5g

Orange Glazed Duck Breast

Prep Time: 15 mins Cooking Time: 20 mins Servings: 2
Ingredients:
2 duck breasts
Zest and juice of 1 orange
2 tablespoons honey
1 tablespoon soy sauce
1 clove garlic, minced
Salt and black pepper to taste
Directions:
Preheat your air fryer to 375°F (190°C).
Score the skin of the duck breasts in a crisscross pattern without cutting into the meat.
In a bowl, whisk together the orange zest, orange juice, honey, soy sauce, minced garlic, salt, and black pepper to create the glaze.
Brush the duck breasts with the glaze, ensuring that the skin is well coated. Place the duck breasts in the air fryer basket, skin-side up.
Air fry for 18-20 mins, until the skin is crispy and the duck is cooked to your desired level of doneness. Check for doneness (internal temperature should be around 130-135°F or 54-57°C for medium-rare).
Allow the duck breasts to rest for a few mins before slicing and serving.
Nutritional Values (per serving): Calories: 358 kcal Protein: 25g Carbohydrates: 14g Fat: 22g Fiber: 1g

Tandoori Chicken Tikka

Prep Time: 20 mins Marinating Time: 1-2 hrs Cooking Time: 15 mins   Servings: 4
Ingredients:
1 pound boneless, skinless chicken breast, cut into bite-sized pieces
1/2 cup plain yogurt
2 tablespoons tandoori masala spice blend
1 tablespoon lemon juice
1 teaspoon fresh ginger, grated
1 teaspoon fresh garlic, minced
Salt and black pepper to taste
Naan bread and yogurt-based sauce (if desired)
Skewers, wooden or metal (if using wooden skewers, soak them in water for 30 mins)
Directions:
In a bowl, combine grated ginger, minced garlic, plain yogurt, tandoori masala spice blend, lemon juice, salt, and black pepper to create the marinade.

Add the chicken pieces to the marinade, ensuring they are well coated. Cover and refrigerate for 1-2 hrs. Preheat your air fryer to 375°F.
Thread the marinated chicken pieces onto skewers. Place the chicken skewers in the air fryer basket in a single layer.
Air fry for 12-15 mins, turning the skewers halfway through, until the chicken is cooked through and has a charred appearance.
Check for doneness (internal temperature should be 165°F or 74°C).
Serve the tandoori chicken tikka with naan bread and yogurt-based sauce if desired.
Nutritional Values (per serving): Calories: 187 kcal Protein: 25g Carbohydrates: 4g Fat: 6g Fiber: 1g

Pesto and Mozzarella Stuffed Turkey Meatballs

Prep Time: 20 mins Cooking Time: 15 mins Servings: 4
Ingredients:
1 pound ground turkey
1/4 cup breadcrumbs
1/4 cup grated Parmesan cheese
1/4 cup basil pesto
4 small mozzarella cheese balls (or cubes)
1 teaspoon garlic powder
1/2 teaspoon dried basil
Salt and black pepper to taste
Marinara sauce (for serving, optional)
Directions:
Preheat your air fryer to 375°F (190°C).
In a bowl, combine ground turkey, breadcrumbs, grated Parmesan cheese, garlic powder, dried basil, salt, and black pepper.
Divide the turkey mixture into 4 equal portions.
Take one portion and flatten it in your hand. Place a mozzarella cheese ball in the center and shape the turkey mixture around it to form a meatball. Repeat for the remaining portions.
Place the stuffed turkey meatballs in the air fryer basket.
Air fry for 12-15 mins, until the meatballs are cooked through and the cheese is melted.
Check for doneness (internal temperature should be 165°F or 74°C).
Serve the meatballs with marinara sauce if desired.
Nutritional Values (per serving, without marinara sauce): Calories: 291 kcal Protein: 28g Carbohydrates: 8g Fat: 16g Fiber: 1g

Crispy Coconut Shrimp

Prep Time: 20 mins Cooking Time: 10 mins
Servings: 4
Ingredients:
1 pound large shrimp, peeled and deveined
1/2 cup shredded coconut
1/2 cup panko breadcrumbs
1/4 cup all-purpose flour
2 large eggs, beaten
Salt and black pepper to taste
Cooking spray
Sweet chili sauce (for dipping, optional)

Directions:
Preheat your air fryer to 375°F (190°C).
In a shallow dish, combine shredded coconut, panko breadcrumbs, and a pinch of salt.
Place the flour in another shallow dish and season it with a bit of salt and black pepper.
Dip each shrimp in the flour to coat, then in the beaten eggs, and finally in the coconut-breadcrumb mixture, pressing the coating onto the shrimp to adhere.
Place the coated shrimp in the air fryer basket in a single layer.
Lightly spray the shrimp with cooking spray to help them get crispy.
Air fry for 8-10 mins, turning them halfway through, until the shrimp are golden brown and cooked through.
Serve the crispy coconut shrimp with sweet chili sauce for dipping if desired.
Nutritional Values (per serving, without sauce):
Calories: 271 kcal Protein: 22g Carbohydrates: 18g Fat: 13g Fiber: 2g

Lemon Garlic Butter Scallops

Prep Time: 10 mins Cooking Time: 5 mins
Servings: 4
Ingredients:
1 pound large scallops
2 tablespoons unsalted butter
2 cloves garlic, minced
Zest and juice of 1 lemon
Salt and black pepper to taste
Fresh parsley, chopped (for garnish)

Directions:
Preheat your air fryer to 375°F (190°C).
Pat the scallops dry with paper towels and season them with a pinch of salt and black pepper.
In a microwave-safe bowl, melt the butter and then mix in the minced garlic, lemon zest, and lemon juice.
Brush each scallop with the lemon garlic butter mixture.
Place the scallops in the air fryer basket in a single layer.
Air fry for 4-5 mins, until the scallops are opaque and just cooked through.
Check for doneness (scallops should be slightly firm to the touch).
Garnish with chopped fresh parsley before serving.
Nutritional Values (per serving): Calories: 158 kcal Protein: 20g Carbohydrates: 3g Fat: 6g Fiber: 0.5g

Crispy Lemon Pepper Chicken Wings

Prep Time: 15 mins Cooking Time: 25 mins
Servings: 4
Ingredients:
2 pounds chicken wings
2 tablespoons olive oil
1 tablespoon lemon pepper seasoning
1/2 teaspoon garlic powder
1/2 teaspoon onion powder
Salt to taste
Lemon wedges (for serving)

Directions:
Preheat your air fryer to 400°F (200°C).
In a large bowl, toss the chicken wings with olive oil, lemon pepper seasoning, garlic powder, onion powder, and salt.
Place the seasoned chicken wings in the air fryer basket.
Air fry for 20-25 mins, shaking the basket or flipping the wings halfway through, until they are crispy and cooked through.
Serve with lemon wedges for squeezing over the wings.
Nutritional Values (per serving): Calories: 334 kcal Protein: 26g Carbohydrates: 8g Fat: 27g Fiber: 0g

Herbed Garlic Butter Turkey Breast

Prep Time: 15 mins Cooking Time: 30 mins
Servings: 4
Ingredients:
1 boneless turkey breast (about 2 pounds)
4 tablespoons unsalted butter, softened
2 cloves garlic, minced
1 teaspoon dried thyme
1 teaspoon dried rosemary
Salt and black pepper to taste

Directions:
Preheat your air fryer to 375°F (190°C).
In a bowl, mix together the softened butter, minced garlic, dried thyme, dried rosemary, salt, and black pepper.
Spread the herbed butter mixture all over the turkey breast.
Place the turkey breast in the air fryer basket.
Air fry for 25-30 mins, until the turkey is cooked through and the skin is golden brown.
Check for doneness (internal temperature should be 165°F or 74°C).
Allow the turkey breast to rest for a few mins before slicing.
Nutritional Values (per serving): Calories: 258 kcal Protein: 35g Carbohydrates: 6g Fat: 12g Fiber: 0g

BBQ Turkey Burgers

Prep Time: 15 mins Cooking Time: 15 mins
Servings: 4
Ingredients:
1 pound ground turkey
1/4 cup BBQ sauce (your favorite brand)
1/4 cup breadcrumbs
1/4 cup grated cheddar cheese
1/2 teaspoon smoked paprika
Salt and black pepper to taste
Hamburger buns and your choice of toppings (lettuce, tomato, onion, etc.)

Directions:
Preheat your air fryer to 375°F (190°C).
In a bowl, combine ground turkey, BBQ sauce, breadcrumbs, grated cheddar cheese, smoked paprika, salt, and black pepper.

Shape the mixture into four turkey burger patties. Place the turkey burger patties in the air fryer basket.
Air fry for 12-15 mins, flipping the burgers halfway through, until they are cooked through.
Check for doneness (internal temperature should be 165°F or 74°C).
Serve the BBQ turkey burgers on hamburger buns with your favorite toppings.
Nutritional Values (per serving, without toppings): Calories: 262 kcal Protein: 25g Carbohydrates: 15g Fat: 10g Fiber: 1g

Cajun Spiced Turkey Drumsticks

Prep Time: 15 mins Cooking Time: 25 mins
Servings: 4
Ingredients:
8 turkey drumsticks
2 tablespoons Cajun seasoning
2 tablespoons olive oil
1 teaspoon garlic powder
1 teaspoon onion powder
Salt and black pepper to taste
Lemon wedges (for serving)
Directions:
Preheat your air fryer to 375°F (190°C).
In a bowl, mix the Cajun seasoning, olive oil, garlic powder, onion powder, salt, and black pepper.
Coat the turkey drumsticks evenly with the Cajun spice mixture.
Place the drumsticks in the air fryer basket.
Air fry for 20-25 mins, flipping them halfway through, until they are cooked through and have a crispy exterior. Check for doneness (internal temperature should be 165°F or 74°C).
Serve the Cajun spiced turkey drumsticks with lemon wedges for a zesty twist.
Nutritional Values (per serving): Calories: 307 kcal Protein: 30g Carbohydrates: 2g Fat: 18g Fiber: 0.5g

Thai Basil Chicken Stir-Fry

Prep Time: 15 mins Cooking Time: 10 mins
Servings: 4
Ingredients:
1 pound boneless, skinless chicken breasts, thinly sliced
2 tablespoons soy sauce
1 tablespoon fish sauce
1 tablespoon oyster sauce
1 teaspoon brown sugar
2 cloves garlic, minced
1 red chili pepper, thinly sliced (adjust to your spice preference)
1 cup fresh basil leaves
1 tablespoon vegetable oil
Cooked jasmine rice (for serving)

Directions:
In a bowl, mix together soy sauce, fish sauce, oyster sauce, and brown sugar to create the sauce.
Heat vegetable oil in a skillet or wok over high heat.
Add minced garlic and sliced chicken to the hot pan and stir-fry until the chicken is cooked through.
Pour the sauce over the cooked chicken and stir well.
Add the sliced chili pepper and fresh basil leaves, continuing to stir-fry until the basil wilts.
Serve the Thai basil chicken stir-fry over cooked jasmine rice.
Nutritional Values (per serving, without rice): Calories: 205 kcal Protein: 25g Carbohydrates: 4g Fat: 9g Fiber: 1g

Buffalo Chicken Tenders

Prep Time: 15 mins Cooking Time: 12 mins
Servings: 4
Ingredients:
1 pound chicken tenders
1/2 cup hot sauce (your favorite brand)
1/4 cup unsalted butter, melted
1/2 teaspoon garlic powder
1/2 teaspoon onion powder
Cooking spray
Ranch or blue cheese dressing (for dipping, optional)
Celery sticks (for serving, optional)

Directions:
Preheat your air fryer to 400°F (200°C).

In a bowl, combine hot sauce, melted butter, garlic powder, and onion powder to create the buffalo sauce.
Dip each chicken tender into the buffalo sauce to coat and place them in the air fryer basket.
Lightly spray the chicken tenders with cooking spray for extra crispiness.
Air fry for 10-12 mins, flipping the tenders halfway through, until they are crispy and cooked through.
Serve the buffalo chicken tenders with ranch or blue cheese dressing and optional celery sticks.
Nutritional Values (per serving, without dressing or celery): Calories: 309 kcal Protein: 25g Carbohydrates: 15g Fat: 21g Fiber: 0g

Honey Sriracha Chicken Thighs

Prep Time: 15 mins Cooking Time: 20 mins
Servings: 4
Ingredients:
4 bone-in, skin-on chicken thighs
1/4 cup honey
2 tablespoons Sriracha sauce (adjust to your spice preference)
2 tablespoons soy sauce
1 tablespoon rice vinegar
1 teaspoon garlic powder
1/2 teaspoon grated ginger
Salt and black pepper to taste
Directions:
Preheat your air fryer to 375°F (190°C).
In a bowl, whisk together honey, Sriracha sauce, soy sauce, rice vinegar, garlic powder, grated ginger, salt, and black pepper to create the glaze.
Brush the chicken thighs with the honey Sriracha glaze, making sure to coat them well.
Place the chicken thighs in the air fryer basket, skin-side up.
Air fry for 18-20 mins, until the chicken is cooked through and the skin is crispy.
Check for doneness (internal temperature should be 165°F or 74°C).
Serve the honey Sriracha chicken thighs with your choice of side dishes.
Nutritional Values (per serving): Calories: 349 kcal Protein: 24g Carbohydrates: 20g Fat: 18g

CHAPTER 6
BEEF RECIPES

Air Fryer Steak

Prep Time: 10 mins   Cooking Time: 10 mins
Servings: 2
Ingredients:
2 beef steaks (e.g., ribeye, sirloin)
2 tablespoons olive oil
1 teaspoon salt
1/2 teaspoon black pepper
1/2 teaspoon garlic powder
1/2 teaspoon dried rosemary (optional)

Directions:
Preheat your air fryer to 400°F (200°C).
Rub both sides of the steaks with olive oil, salt, black pepper, garlic powder, and dried rosemary.
Place the steaks in the air fryer basket.
Air fry for 8-10 mins for medium-rare, flipping them halfway through.
Adjust the cooking time for your desired level of doneness.
Let the steaks rest for a few mins before slicing and serving.
Nutritional Values (per serving): Calories: 371 kcal Protein: 30g Carbohydrates: 7g Fat: 24g Fiber: 0g

Air Fryer Beef Kebabs

Prep Time: 20 mins   Cooking Time: 12 mins
Servings: 4
Ingredients:
1 pound beef sirloin, cubed
1 red bell pepper, cut into chunks
1 green bell pepper, cut into chunks
1 red onion, cut into chunks
2 tablespoons olive oil
2 tablespoons soy sauce
1 teaspoon garlic powder
1 teaspoon dried oregano
Salt and black pepper to taste
Wooden skewers (soaked in water for 30 mins)

Directions:
Preheat your air fryer to 375°F (190°C).

In a bowl, mix together olive oil, soy sauce, garlic powder, dried oregano, salt, and black pepper.
Thread beef cubes, bell pepper chunks, and red onion onto wooden skewers, alternating as desired.
Brush the skewers with the olive oil mixture.
Place the skewers in the air fryer basket.
Air fry for 10-12 mins, turning them halfway through, until the beef is cooked to your desired level of doneness.
Serve the beef kebabs with your favorite dipping sauce.
Nutritional Values (per serving): Calories: 283 kcal Protein: 24g Carbohydrates: 6g Fat: 18g Fiber: 2g

Air Fryer Beef and Broccoli

Prep Time: 15 mins   Cooking Time: 10 mins
Servings: 4
Ingredients:
1 pound beef sirloin, thinly sliced
2 cups broccoli florets
1/4 cup soy sauce
2 tablespoons oyster sauce
2 tablespoons brown sugar
2 cloves garlic, minced
1/2 teaspoon ginger, grated
1 tablespoon cornstarch
Cooked rice (for serving)

Directions:
In a small bowl, whisk together soy sauce, oyster sauce, brown sugar, minced garlic, grated ginger, and cornstarch. Set aside.
Preheat your air fryer to 400°F (200°C).
Place the beef slices and broccoli florets in the air fryer basket. Air fry for 5 mins.
Remove the basket, stir the beef and broccoli, and pour the sauce over them.
Return the basket to the air fryer and air fry for another 5 mins.
Serve the beef and broccoli over cooked rice.
Nutritional Values (per serving): Calories: 324 kcal Protein: 26g Carbohydrates: 22g Fat: 13g Fiber: 2g

Air Fryer Beef and Vegetable Stir-Fry

Prep Time: 20 mins   Cooking Time: 10 mins
Servings: 4
Ingredients:
1 pound beef sirloin, thinly sliced
2 cups mixed vegetables (broccoli, bell peppers, snap peas, carrots, etc.), sliced
2 tablespoons soy sauce
1 tablespoon oyster sauce
1 tablespoon brown sugar
2 cloves garlic, minced
1/2 teaspoon ginger, grated
Salt and black pepper to taste
Cooked rice or noodles (for serving)
Directions:
In a bowl, combine soy sauce, oyster sauce, brown sugar, minced garlic, grated ginger, salt, and black pepper. Set aside. Preheat your air fryer to 375°F.
Place the beef slices and mixed vegetables in the air fryer basket.
Air fry for 8-10 mins, shaking the basket occasionally, until the beef is cooked and the vegetables are tender-crisp.
Remove the basket, pour the sauce over the beef and vegetables, and toss to coat.
Serve the beef and vegetable stir-fry over cooked rice or noodles.
Nutritional Values (per serving without rice/noodles): Calories: 284 kcal Protein: 26g Carbohydrates: 12g Fat: 14g Fiber: 3g

Air Fryer Beef and Mushroom Wellington

Prep Time: 30 mins   Cooking Time: 20 mins
Servings: 4
Ingredients:
4 beef tenderloin steaks
2 sheets puff pastry, thawed
1 cup mushrooms, finely chopped
1/2 onion, finely chopped
2 cloves garlic, minced
2 tablespoons olive oil
2 tablespoons Dijon mustard
Salt and black pepper to taste
1 egg (for egg wash)
Directions:
Preheat your air fryer to 375°F (190°C).

In a skillet over medium heat, sauté mushrooms, onions, and garlic in olive oil until the mixture is soft and the liquid from the mushrooms has evaporated. Season with salt and black pepper. Set aside to cool.
Season the beef steaks with salt and black pepper. Spread a thin layer of Dijon mustard on each steak. Divide the mushroom mixture among the steaks, placing it on top of the mustard.
Roll out each sheet of puff pastry and cut it into squares large enough to encase each steak.
Place a steak in the center of each pastry square. Fold the pastry over the steak, sealing the edges with egg wash.
Place the wrapped steaks in the air fryer basket.
Air fry for 15-20 mins until the pastry is golden brown and the beef is cooked to your desired doneness.
Let them rest for a few mins before serving.
Nutritional Values (per serving): Calories: 447 kcal Protein: 30g Carbohydrates: 28g Fat: 25g Fiber: 2g

Air Fryer Beef and Potato Tacos

Prep Time: 20 mins   Cooking Time: 15 mins
Servings: 4
Ingredients:
1 pound ground beef
2 cups diced potatoes
1/2 onion, diced
1 red bell pepper, diced
2 cloves garlic, minced
1 teaspoon chili powder
1/2 teaspoon cumin
1/2 teaspoon paprika
Salt and black pepper to taste
8 small taco shells or tortillas
Directions:
In a skillet over medium heat, cook ground beef until browned. Drain excess fat.
Add diced potatoes and cook until they begin to soften. Add diced onions, diced red bell pepper, and minced garlic. Continue to cook until the vegetables are tender.
Stir in chili powder, cumin, paprika, salt, and black pepper. Preheat your air fryer to 375°F (190°C).
Place the beef and potato mixture in the air fryer basket.
Air fry for 15 mins, stirring occasionally, until the potatoes are crispy and browned.
Warm the taco shells or tortillas according to package. Then serve
Nutrition values: calories 325kcal protein: 21g carbohydrates: 11g Fiber: 2g

Air Fryer Beef and Cheese Stuffed Poblano Peppers

Prep Time: 25 mins   Cooking Time: 20 mins
Servings: 4
Ingredients:
4 poblano peppers
1 pound ground beef
1/2 onion, finely chopped
2 cloves garlic, minced
1 teaspoon chili powder
1/2 teaspoon cumin
1/2 teaspoon oregano
Salt and black pepper to taste
1 cup shredded Monterey Jack cheese
Salsa and sour cream (for serving)
Directions:
Preheat your air fryer to 375°F (190°C). Cut a slit lengthwise along each poblano pepper, leaving them whole. Remove seeds and membranes.
In a skillet over medium heat, cook ground beef until browned. Drain excess fat.
Add chopped onions and minced garlic to the skillet. Cook until onions are translucent.
Stir in chili powder, cumin, oregano, salt, and black pepper. Fill each poblano pepper with the beef mixture and top with shredded Monterey Jack cheese. Place the stuffed poblano peppers in the air fryer basket. Air fry for 15-20 mins until the peppers are tender and the cheese is melted and bubbly. Serve with salsa and sour cream on the side.
Nutritional Values (per serving): Calories: 343 kcal Protein: 26g Carbohydrates: 11g Fat: 22g Fiber: 3g

Air Fryer Beef and Onion Stuffed Potatoes

Prep Time: 30 mins   Cooking Time: 30 mins
Servings: 4
Ingredients:
4 large russet potatoes
1 pound ground beef
1/2 onion, finely chopped
2 cloves garlic, minced
1/2 cup shredded cheddar cheese
1/4 cup sour cream
2 tablespoons butter
Salt and black pepper to taste
Chopped fresh chives (for garnish)
Directions:

Preheat your air fryer to 400°F (200°C).
Pierce the potatoes with a fork in several places and microwave them on high for 10 mins or until they are slightly softened.
In a skillet over medium heat, cook ground beef until browned. Drain excess fat.
Add chopped onions and minced garlic to the skillet. Cook until onions are translucent.
Cut a slit lengthwise in each potato and gently scoop out some of the flesh to create a well.
Mash the removed potato flesh with sour cream, butter, salt, and black pepper.
Fill each potato with the mashed potato mixture and top with the beef and onion mixture. Place the stuffed potatoes in the air fryer basket. Air fry for 25-30 mins until the potatoes are crispy on the outside.
Top with shredded cheddar cheese and air fry for an additional 2 mins until the cheese is melted. Garnish with chopped fresh chives before serving.
Nutritional Values (per serving): Calories: 487 kcal Protein: 23g Carbohydrates: 47g Fat: 23g Fiber: 5g

Air Fryer Beef and Bean Burritos

Prep Time: 20 mins   Cooking Time: 10 mins
Servings: 4
Ingredients:
1 pound ground beef
1 packet taco seasoning mix
1 can (15 ounces) refried beans
4 large flour tortillas
1 cup shredded cheddar cheese
Chopped lettuce, diced tomatoes, and sour cream (for topping)
Directions:
In a skillet over medium heat, cook ground beef until browned. Drain excess fat. Add the taco seasoning mix and water according to package directions. Simmer for a few mins.
Warm the refried beans in a microwave or on the stove. Lay out a tortilla and spread a portion of refried beans down the center. Add the beef mixture and top with shredded cheddar cheese.
Fold in the sides of the tortilla and then roll it up to create a burrito.
Preheat your air fryer to 375°F (190°C). Place the burritos in the air fryer basket. Air fry for 5-7 mins until the burritos are crispy and heated through.
Serve with chopped lettuce, diced tomatoes, and sour cream.
Nutritional Values (per serving): Calories: 522 kcal Protein: 30g Carbohydrates: 36g Fat: 29g Fiber: 6g

Beef and Black Bean Quesadillas

Prep Time: 15 mins   Cooking Time: 8 mins
Servings: 4
Ingredients:
1/2 pound ground beef
1/2 cup canned black beans, drained and rinsed
1 cup shredded Monterey Jack cheese
4 large flour tortillas
Cooking spray
Salsa and sour cream (for dipping, optional)
Directions:
In a skillet over medium heat, cook ground beef until browned. Drain excess fat.
Stir in the black beans and cook for a few more mins until heated through.
Preheat your air fryer to 375°F (190°C).
Lay out a tortilla and sprinkle with shredded Monterey Jack cheese.
Add a portion of the beef and black bean mixture on top of the cheese.
Top with another tortilla to create a quesadilla.
Lightly spray both sides of the quesadilla with cooking spray.
Place the quesadilla in the air fryer basket.
Air fry for 4 mins, flip the quesadilla, and air fry for another 4 mins until it's crispy and the cheese is melted.
Repeat for additional quesadillas if needed.
Serve with salsa and sour cream for dipping, if desired.
Nutritional Values (per serving): Calories: 451 kcal Protein: 24g Carbohydrates: 28g Fat: 25g Fiber: 4g

Air Fryer Beef and Spinach Stuffed Mushrooms

Prep Time: 20 mins   Cooking Time: 10 mins
Servings: 4
Ingredients:
16 large mushroom caps, stems removed
1/2 pound ground beef
1/2 cup spinach, chopped
1/4 cup cream cheese
1/4 cup grated Parmesan cheese
1/4 cup breadcrumbs
2 cloves garlic, minced
2 tablespoons olive oil
Salt and black pepper to taste
Chopped fresh parsley (for garnish)
Directions:
Preheat your air fryer to 375°F (190°C).

In a skillet over medium heat, cook ground beef until browned. Drain excess fat.
Add chopped spinach and minced garlic to the skillet. Cook until spinach is wilted.
Stir in cream cheese, Parmesan cheese, breadcrumbs, salt, and black pepper. Cook until well combined.
Fill each mushroom cap with the beef and spinach mixture. Brush the outside of each mushroom cap with olive oil.
Place the stuffed mushrooms in the air fryer basket.
Air fry for 8-10 mins until the mushrooms are tender and the filling is heated through.
Garnish with chopped fresh parsley before serving.
Nutritional Values (per serving): Calories: 260 kcal Protein: 17g Carbohydrates: 8g Fat: 17g Fiber: 2g

Air Fryer Beef and Cheese Stuffed Zucchini Boats

Prep Time: 20 mins   Cooking Time: 15 mins
Servings: 4
Ingredients:
2 large zucchini
1 pound ground beef
1/2 onion, finely chopped
2 cloves garlic, minced
1 cup marinara sauce
1 cup shredded mozzarella cheese
1/4 cup grated Parmesan cheese
Salt and black pepper to taste
Chopped fresh basil (for garnish)
Directions:
Preheat your air fryer to 375°F (190°C).
Cut each zucchini in half lengthwise and scoop out the seeds to create "boats."
In a skillet over medium heat, cook ground beef until browned. Drain excess fat.
Add chopped onions and minced garlic to the skillet. Cook until onions are translucent.
Stir in marinara sauce, salt, and black pepper. Simmer for a few mins.
Fill each zucchini boat with the beef and sauce mixture.
Top with shredded mozzarella cheese and grated Parmesan cheese.
Place the stuffed zucchini boats in the air fryer basket. Air fry for 12-15 mins until the zucchini is tender, and the cheese is melted and bubbly.
Garnish with chopped fresh basil before serving.
Nutritional Values (per serving): Calories: 386 kcal Protein: 26g Carbohydrates: 10g Fat: 26g Fiber: 2g

Beef and Potato Croquettes

Prep Time: 25 mins   Cooking Time: 15 mins
Servings: 4
Ingredients:
1 pound ground beef
2 cups mashed potatoes
1/2 onion, finely chopped
2 cloves garlic, minced
1/4 cup bread crumbs
1/4 cup grated Parmesan cheese
1/4 cup chopped fresh parsley
1 egg, beaten
Salt and black pepper to taste
Cooking spray
Directions:
In a skillet over medium heat, cook ground beef until browned. Drain excess fat.
Add chopped onions and minced garlic to the skillet. Cook until onions are translucent.
In a large bowl, combine the cooked ground beef, mashed potatoes, bread crumbs, grated Parmesan cheese, chopped parsley, beaten egg, salt, and black pepper.
Shape the mixture into croquettes or patties.
Preheat your air fryer to 375°F (190°C).
Lightly coat the croquettes with cooking spray.
Place the croquettes in the air fryer basket.
Air fry for 12-15 mins until they are golden brown and heated through. Serve hot.
Nutritional Values (per serving): Calories: 377 kcal Protein: 22g Carbohydrates: 25g Fat: 21g Fiber: 3g

Beef and Potato Skewers

Prep Time: 20 mins   Cooking Time: 15 mins
Servings: 4
Ingredients:
1 pound beef sirloin, cut into cubes
2 cups baby potatoes, boiled and halved
1/2 red onion, cut into chunks
1 red bell pepper, cut into chunks
2 cloves garlic, minced
2 tablespoons olive oil
1 teaspoon smoked paprika
1/2 teaspoon dried thyme
Salt and black pepper to taste
Wooden skewers (soaked in water for 30 mins)

Directions:

In a bowl, combine olive oil, minced garlic, smoked paprika, dried thyme, salt, and black pepper.
Thread beef cubes, halved baby potatoes, red onion chunks, and red bell pepper chunks onto wooden skewers.
Brush the skewers with the olive oil mixture.
Preheat your air fryer to 375°F (190°C).
Place the skewers in the air fryer basket.
Air fry for 12-15 mins, turning them halfway through, until the beef is cooked to your desired level of doneness and the vegetables are tender.
Serve the beef and potato skewers hot.
Nutritional Values (per serving): Calories: 374 kcal Protein: 21g Carbohydrates: 22g Fat: 19g Fiber: 3g

Fryer Beef and Corn Fritters

Prep Time: 20 mins   Cooking Time: 10 mins
Servings: 4
Ingredients:
1/2 pound ground beef
1 cup canned corn kernels, drained
1/2 cup flour
1/4 cup milk
1 egg
1/4 cup diced bell peppers (any color)
1/4 cup diced onions
1/4 teaspoon chili powder
Salt and black pepper to taste
Cooking spray
Directions:
In a skillet over medium heat, cook ground beef until browned. Drain excess fat.
In a large bowl, combine cooked ground beef, canned corn kernels, flour, milk, egg, diced bell peppers, diced onions, chili powder, salt, and black pepper. Mix until well combined.
Preheat your air fryer to 375°F (190°C).
Form the mixture into small patties or fritters.
Lightly coat both sides of the fritters with cooking spray.
Place the fritters in the air fryer basket.
Air fry for 8-10 mins until they are golden brown and cooked through.
Serve the beef and corn fritters hot with your favorite dipping sauce.
Nutritional Values (per serving): Calories: 392 kcal Protein: 20g Carbohydrates: 20g Fat: 17g Fiber: 2g

CHAPTER 7
PORK RECIPES

Air Fryer Pork Chops

Prep Time: 10 mins   Cooking Time: 12 mins
Servings: 2
Ingredients:
2 boneless pork chops
1 tablespoon olive oil
1 teaspoon garlic powder
1 teaspoon paprika
1/2 teaspoon dried thyme
Salt and black pepper to taste
Directions:
Preheat your air fryer to 375°F (190°C).
Rub both sides of the pork chops with olive oil.
In a small bowl, mix together garlic powder, paprika, dried thyme, salt, and black pepper.
Season both sides of the pork chops with the spice mixture.
Place the pork chops in the air fryer basket.
Air fry for 10-12 mins, flipping them halfway through, until they reach an internal temperature of 145°F (63°C).
Let the pork chops rest for a few mins before serving.
Nutritional Values (per serving): Calories: 244 kcal Protein: 25g Carbohydrates: 1g Fat: 16g Fiber: 0g

BBQ Pulled Pork Sliders

Prep Time: 15 mins   Cooking Time: 20 mins
Servings: 4
Ingredients:
1 pound boneless pork shoulder or pork butt
1/2 cup BBQ sauce
1/4 cup water
1 teaspoon garlic powder
1 teaspoon onion powder
1/2 teaspoon smoked paprika
1/4 teaspoon cayenne pepper (optional)
Slider buns
Coleslaw (optional, for topping)
Directions:
In a bowl, mix together BBQ sauce, water, garlic powder, onion powder, smoked paprika, and cayenne pepper (if using).

Place the pork shoulder or pork butt in the air fryer basket.
Pour the BBQ sauce mixture over the pork.
Preheat your air fryer to 375°F (190°C).
Air fry for 20-25 mins per pound, flipping and basting the pork with the sauce every 10 mins, until it's tender and shreds easily.
Shred the pork using two forks.
Serve the pulled pork on slider buns, topped with coleslaw if desired.
Nutritional Values (excluding coleslaw): Calories: 309 kcal Protein: 25g Carbohydrates: 25g Fat: 10g Fiber: 1g

Pork Tenderloin with Herb Crust

Prep Time: 15 mins   Cooking Time: 25 mins
Servings: 4
Ingredients:
1 pork tenderloin (about 1 pound)
2 tablespoons Dijon mustard
1 cup breadcrumbs
2 tablespoons grated Parmesan cheese
1 teaspoon dried thyme
1 teaspoon dried rosemary
Salt and black pepper to taste
Cooking spray

Directions:
Preheat your air fryer to 375°F (190°C).
Rub the pork tenderloin with Dijon mustard, coating it evenly.
In a bowl, combine breadcrumbs, grated Parmesan cheese, dried thyme, dried rosemary, salt, and black pepper.
Roll the mustard-coated pork tenderloin in the breadcrumb mixture, pressing the breadcrumbs onto the surface to form a crust.
Lightly coat the pork with cooking spray.
Place the pork tenderloin in the air fryer basket.
Air fry for 20-25 mins, turning it once halfway through, until the internal temperature reaches 145°F (63°C) and the crust is golden brown.
Let it rest for a few mins before slicing and serving.
Nutritional Values (per serving): Calories: 283 kcal Protein: 30g Carbohydrates: 15g Fat: 10g Fiber: 1g

Pork and Pineapple Skewers

Prep Time: 20 mins   Cooking Time: 10 mins
Servings: 4
Ingredients:
1 pound pork loin or tenderloin, cut into cubes
1 cup pineapple chunks (fresh or canned)
1/4 cup soy sauce
2 tablespoons honey
2 tablespoons olive oil
1 teaspoon garlic powder
1/2 teaspoon ground ginger
Salt and black pepper to taste
Wooden skewers (soaked in water for 30 mins)
Directions:
In a bowl, whisk together soy sauce, honey, olive oil, garlic powder, ground ginger, salt, and black pepper.
Thread pork cubes and pineapple chunks alternately onto wooden skewers.
Place the skewers in a shallow dish and pour the marinade over them. Let them marinate for 15 mins.
Preheat your air fryer to 375°F (190°C).
Place the skewers in the air fryer basket, leaving space between them.
Air fry for 8-10 mins, turning the skewers halfway through, until the pork is cooked through and slightly caramelized.
Serve the pork and pineapple skewers hot.
Nutritional Values (per serving): Calories: 292 kcal Protein: 24g Carbohydrates: 20g Fat: 12g Fiber: 1g

Pork Schnitzel

Prep Time: 15 mins   Cooking Time: 10 mins
Servings: 4
Ingredients:
4 boneless pork chops
1 cup breadcrumbs
1/2 cup all-purpose flour
2 eggs, beaten
1 teaspoon paprika
1/2 teaspoon garlic powder
1/2 teaspoon dried thyme
Salt and black pepper to taste
Cooking spray
Lemon wedges (for serving)
Directions:
Preheat your air fryer to 400°F (200°C).

In a shallow dish, combine breadcrumbs, paprika, garlic powder, dried thyme, salt, and black pepper. Place the flour in another shallow dish and the beaten eggs in a third shallow dish.
Dredge each pork chop in the flour, shaking off excess, then dip it into the beaten eggs, and finally coat it with the breadcrumb mixture, pressing the breadcrumbs.
Lightly coat both sides of the breaded pork chops with cooking spray. Place the breaded pork chops in the air fryer basket.
Air fry for 5-7 mins on each side at 400°F (200°C) until they are golden brown and crispy, and the internal temperature reaches 145°F (63°C).
Remove the pork schnitzel from the air fryer and place them on paper towels to drain excess oil.
Serve hot with lemon wedges for a zesty touch.
Nutritional Values (per serving): Calories: 326 kcal Protein: 28g Carbohydrates: 27g Fat: 11g Fiber: 2g

Pork and Vegetable Stir-Fry

Prep Time: 20 mins   Cooking Time: 10 mins
Servings: 4
Ingredients:
1 pound pork loin, thinly sliced
2 cups mixed vegetables (bell peppers, broccoli, snap peas, carrots, etc.), sliced
2 tablespoons soy sauce
1 tablespoon hoisin sauce
1 tablespoon honey
2 cloves garlic, minced
1/2 teaspoon ginger, grated
Salt and black pepper to taste
Cooked rice (for serving)
Directions:
In a bowl, combine soy sauce, hoisin sauce, honey, minced garlic, grated ginger, salt, and black pepper. Set aside.
Preheat your air fryer to 375°F (190°C).
Place the sliced pork and mixed vegetables in the air fryer basket.
Air fry for 8-10 mins, shaking the basket occasionally, until the pork is cooked and the vegetables are tender-crisp.
Remove the basket, pour the sauce over the pork and vegetables, and toss to coat.
Serve the pork and vegetable stir-fry over cooked rice.
Nutritional Values (per serving without rice): Calories: 243 kcal Protein: 24g Carbohydrates: 18g Fat: 8g Fiber: 3g

Pork and Mushroom Risotto

Prep Time: 15 mins   Cooking Time: 25 mins
Servings: 4
Ingredients:
1 pound boneless pork loin, cut into cubes
1 cup Arborio rice
1/2 cup sliced mushrooms
1/2 cup diced onions
2 cloves garlic, minced
4 cups chicken broth
1/2 cup dry white wine (optional)
1/4 cup grated Parmesan cheese
2 tablespoons olive oil
Salt and black pepper to taste
Directions:
Preheat your air fryer to 375°F (190°C).
In a skillet over medium heat, heat olive oil and sauté diced onions and minced garlic until translucent.
Add Arborio rice and sliced mushrooms. Cook for a few mins until rice is lightly toasted.
If using white wine, pour it into the skillet and cook until it's mostly absorbed.
Transfer the rice mixture to the air fryer basket.
Place the cubed pork on top of the rice.
Pour in the chicken broth.
Air fry for 20-25 mins, stirring gently every 5 mins, until the rice is creamy and tender.
Stir in grated Parmesan cheese, salt, and black pepper.
Serve the pork and mushroom risotto hot.
Nutritional Values (per serving): Calories: 430 kcal Protein: 26g Carbohydrates: 39g Fat: 16g Fiber: 2g

Air Fryer Pork and Bean Tacos

Prep Time: 20 mins   Cooking Time: 12 mins
Servings: 4
Ingredients:
1 pound ground pork
1 can (15 ounces) black beans, drained and rinsed
1 cup diced tomatoes
1/2 onion, diced
2 cloves garlic, minced
1 teaspoon chili powder
1/2 teaspoon cumin
Salt and black pepper to taste
8 small taco shells or tortillas
Shredded lettuce, diced avocado, and sour cream (for topping)
Directions:
In a skillet over medium heat, cook ground pork until browned. Drain excess fat.

Add diced onions and minced garlic to the skillet. Cook until onions are translucent.
Stir in chili powder, cumin, salt, and black pepper.
Preheat your air fryer to 375°F (190°C). Place the cooked pork mixture in the air fryer basket. Air fry for 5-7 mins, stirring occasionally, until it's heated through.
Warm the taco shells or tortillas according to package instructions. Fill each shell with the pork and bean mixture.
Top with diced tomatoes, shredded lettuce, diced avocado, and sour cream. Serve the pork and bean tacos immediately, garnished with your favorite toppings.
Nutritional Values (per serving, excluding toppings): Calories: 384 kcal Protein: 22g Carbohydrates: 34g Fat: 18g Fiber: 6g

Pork and Broccoli Stir-Fry

Prep Time: 20 mins   Cooking Time: 10 mins
Servings: 4
Ingredients:
1 pound boneless pork loin, thinly sliced
2 cups broccoli florets
1/2 cup sliced bell peppers (any color)
1/2 cup sliced carrots
1/4 cup soy sauce
2 tablespoons hoisin sauce
2 tablespoons honey
2 cloves garlic, minced
1/2 teaspoon grated ginger
2 teaspoons cornstarch
Salt and black pepper to taste
Cooked rice (for serving)
Directions:
In a bowl, whisk together soy sauce, hoisin sauce, honey, minced garlic, grated ginger, cornstarch, salt, and black pepper. Set aside.
Preheat your air fryer to 375°F (190°C).
Place the sliced pork, broccoli florets, sliced bell peppers, and sliced carrots in the air fryer basket.
Air fry for 8-10 mins, tossing the ingredients occasionally, until the pork is cooked through, and the vegetables are tender-crisp.
Pour the sauce mixture over the cooked pork and vegetables in the air fryer. Toss to coat.
Air fry for an additional 2-3 mins until the sauce thickens and coats the pork and vegetables.
Serve the pork and broccoli stir-fry over cooked rice.
Nutritional Values (excluding rice): Calories: 274 kcal Protein: 24g Carbohydrates: 22g Fat: 10g Fiber: 3g

Pork and Apple Stuffed Acorn Squash

Prep Time: 30 mins   Cooking Time: 20 mins
Servings: 4
Ingredients:
2 small acorn squashes, halved and seeds removed
1 pound ground pork
2 apples, diced
1/2 cup diced onions
2 cloves garlic, minced
1/2 teaspoon dried sage
1/2 teaspoon dried thyme
Salt and black pepper to taste
Cooking spray
Maple syrup (for drizzling)
Directions:
Preheat your air fryer to 375°F (190°C).
Lightly coat the inside of the acorn squash halves with cooking spray and season with salt and black pepper.
In a skillet over medium heat, cook ground pork until browned. Drain excess fat.
Add diced apples, diced onions, minced garlic, dried sage, dried thyme, salt, and black pepper to the skillet. Cook until the apples are softened.
Fill each acorn squash half with the pork and apple mixture.
Place the filled acorn squash halves in the air fryer basket.
Air fry for 18-20 mins until the squash is tender, and the filling is heated through.
Drizzle with maple syrup before serving.
Nutritional Values (per serving): Calories: 347 kcal Protein: 18g Carbohydrates: 40g Fat: 14g Fiber: 6g

Pork and Sweet Potato Hash

Prep Time: 20 mins   Cooking Time: 15 mins
Servings: 4
Ingredients:
1 pound ground pork
2 cups diced sweet potatoes
1/2 cup diced bell peppers (any color)
1/2 cup diced onions
1 teaspoon smoked paprika
1/2 teaspoon dried thyme
Salt and black pepper to taste
Cooking spray
Fried or poached eggs (optional, for serving)

Directions:

In a skillet over medium heat, cook ground pork until browned. Drain excess fat.
Add diced sweet potatoes, diced bell peppers, diced onions, smoked paprika, dried thyme, salt, and black pepper to the skillet. Cook until sweet potatoes are tender.
Preheat your air fryer to 375°F (190°C).
Lightly coat the mixture with cooking spray.
Place the pork and sweet potato hash in the air fryer basket. Air fry for 12-15 mins, stirring occasionally, until the hash is heated through and slightly crispy.
Serve hot, optionally topped with fried or poached eggs.
Nutritional Values (excluding eggs): Calories: 321 kcal Protein: 20g Carbohydrates: 20g Fat: 18g Fiber: 3g

Pork and Bean Burritos

Prep Time: 25 mins   Cooking Time: 10 mins
Servings: 4
Ingredients:
1 pound ground pork
1 can (15 ounces) black beans, drained and rinsed
1 cup cooked rice
1/2 cup diced tomatoes
1/2 cup diced onions
2 cloves garlic, minced
1 teaspoon chili powder
1/2 teaspoon cumin
Salt and black pepper to taste
4 large flour tortillas
Shredded cheddar cheese (for filling)
Salsa and sour cream (for topping, optional)
Directions:
In a skillet over medium heat, cook ground pork until browned. Drain excess fat.
Add diced onions and minced garlic to the skillet. Cook until onions are translucent.
Stir in diced tomatoes, black beans, cooked rice, chili powder, cumin, salt, and black pepper.
Preheat your air fryer to 375°F (190°C). Place a portion of the pork and bean mixture and shredded cheddar cheese in the center of each tortilla. Fold in the sides and roll up each tortilla into a burrito.
Place the burritos in the air fryer basket, seam side down. Air fry for 5-7 mins, turning them once halfway through, until they are heated through and slightly crispy.
Serve the pork and bean burritos hot, with salsa and sour cream if desired.
Nutritional Values (excluding toppings): Calories: 465 kcal Protein: 23g Carbohydrates: 52g Fat: 18g Fiber: 8g

Pork and Spinach Stuffed Mushrooms

Prep Time: 20 mins   Cooking Time: 12 mins
Servings: 4
Ingredients:
16 large mushroom caps, stems removed
1/2 pound ground pork
1/2 cup chopped spinach
1/4 cup cream cheese
1/4 cup grated Parmesan cheese
1/4 cup breadcrumbs
2 cloves garlic, minced
Salt and black pepper to taste
Cooking spray
Directions:
Preheat your air fryer to 375°F (190°C). In a skillet over medium heat, cook ground pork until browned. Drain excess fat. Add chopped spinach and minced garlic to the skillet. Cook until spinach is wilted.
Stir in cream cheese, grated Parmesan cheese, breadcrumbs, salt, and black pepper. Cook until well combined.
Fill each mushroom cap with the pork and spinach mixture. Lightly coat the outside of each mushroom cap with cooking spray.
Place the stuffed mushrooms in the air fryer basket.
Air fry for 10-12 mins until the mushrooms are tender and the filling is heated through.
Serve the pork and spinach stuffed mushrooms hot.
Nutritional Values (per serving): Calories: 239 kcal Protein: 15g Carbohydrates: 12g Fat: 15g Fiber: 2g

Pork and Pineapple Tacos

Prep Time: 20 mins   Cooking Time: 10 mins
Servings: 4
Ingredients:
1 pound pork loin or tenderloin, cut into strips
1 cup diced pineapple
1/2 cup diced red bell peppers
1/2 cup diced onions
1/4 cup fresh cilantro, chopped
Juice of 1 lime
1 teaspoon chili powder
1/2 teaspoon cumin
Salt and black pepper to taste
8 small corn or flour tortillas
Sour cream and hot sauce (for topping, optional)
Directions:
In a bowl, mix together diced pineapple, diced red bell peppers, diced onions, chopped cilantro, lime juice, chili powder, cumin, salt, and black pepper.

Set aside.
Preheat your air fryer to 375°F (190°C).
Place the pork strips in the air fryer basket.
Air fry for 6-8 mins until the pork is cooked through and slightly caramelized.
Warm the tortillas according to package instructions. Fill each tortilla with the air-fried pork and top with the pineapple salsa.
Serve the pork and pineapple tacos with sour cream and hot sauce if desired.
Nutritional Values (excluding toppings): Calories: 332 kcal Protein: 25g Carbohydrates: 40g Fat: 7g Fiber: 4g

Pork and Vegetable Spring Rolls

Prep Time: 30 mins   Cooking Time: 12 mins
Servings: 4
Ingredients:
1/2 pound ground pork
1 cup shredded cabbage
1/2 cup shredded carrots
1/2 cup sliced mushrooms
1/4 cup diced onions
2 cloves garlic, minced
1 teaspoon ginger, grated
2 tablespoons soy sauce
1 teaspoon sesame oil
1/2 teaspoon sugar
12 spring roll wrappers
Cooking spray
Sweet chili sauce (for dipping)
Directions:
In a skillet over medium heat, cook ground pork until browned. Drain excess fat.
Add shredded cabbage, shredded carrots, sliced mushrooms, diced onions, minced garlic, and grated ginger to the skillet. Cook until vegetables are tender.
Stir in soy sauce, sesame oil, and sugar. Cook for an additional minute. Remove from heat.
Preheat your air fryer to 375°F (190°C).
Place a spoonful of the pork and vegetable mixture onto a spring roll wrapper. Roll up, folding in the sides, and seal the edge with a bit of water.
Lightly coat each spring roll with cooking spray.
Place the spring rolls in the air fryer basket.
Air fry for 10-12 mins, turning them once halfway through, until they are crispy and golden brown.
Serve the pork and vegetable spring rolls hot with sweet chili sauce for dipping.
Nutritional Values (per serving): Calories: 237 kcal Protein: 12g Carbohydrates: 32g Fat: 7g Fiber: 2g

CHAPTER 8
VEGETABLE AND SIDE DISH RECIPES

Air Fryer Roasted Brussels Sprouts

Prep Time: 10 mins   Cooking Time: 15 mins
Servings: 4
Ingredients:
1 pound Brussels sprouts, trimmed and halved
2 tablespoons olive oil
2 cloves garlic, minced
Salt and black pepper to taste
Grated Parmesan cheese (optional, for topping)

Directions:
In a bowl, toss the halved Brussels sprouts with olive oil, minced garlic, salt, and black pepper.
Preheat your air fryer to 375°F (190°C).
Place the Brussels sprouts in the air fryer basket.
Air fry for 12-15 mins, shaking the basket occasionally, until they are tender and caramelized.
Optionally, sprinkle with grated Parmesan cheese before serving.
Nutritional Values (per serving, without Parmesan): Calories: 80 kcal Protein: 3g Carbohydrates: 9g Fat: 4g Fiber: 3g

Air Fryer Garlic Parmesan Asparagus

Prep Time: 10 mins   Cooking Time: 8 mins
Servings: 4
Ingredients:
1 bunch asparagus, trimmed
2 tablespoons olive oil
2 cloves garlic, minced
1/4 cup grated Parmesan cheese
Salt and black pepper to taste
Lemon wedges (for serving)

Directions:
Toss the trimmed asparagus with olive oil, minced garlic, salt, and black pepper in a bowl.
Preheat your air fryer to 375°F (190°C).
Place the asparagus in the air fryer basket.

Air fry for 6-8 mins until the asparagus is tender and slightly crispy.
Sprinkle with grated Parmesan cheese and air fry for an additional 1-2 mins until the cheese is melted and golden.
Serve with lemon wedges for a zesty touch.
Nutritional Values (per serving): Calories: 85 kcal Protein: 3g Carbohydrates: 4g Fat: 6g Fiber: 2g

Air Fryer Crispy Sweet Potato Fries

Prep Time: 15 mins   Cooking Time: 20 mins
Servings: 4
Ingredients:
2 large sweet potatoes, cut into thin fries
2 tablespoons olive oil
1 teaspoon paprika
1/2 teaspoon garlic powder
1/2 teaspoon cayenne pepper (optional)
Salt and black pepper to taste

Directions:
In a bowl, toss the sweet potato fries with olive oil, paprika, garlic powder, cayenne pepper (if using), salt, and black pepper.
Preheat your air fryer to 375°F (190°C).
Place the sweet potato fries in the air fryer basket, ensuring they are in a single layer.
Air fry for 18-20 mins, shaking the basket occasionally, until the fries are crispy and golden brown.
Serve hot.
Nutritional Values (per serving): Calories: 151 kcal Protein: 2g Carbohydrates: 21g Fat: 7g Fiber: 4g

Garlic Herb Roasted Potatoes

Prep Time: 15 mins   Cooking Time: 20 mins
Servings: 4
Ingredients:
1 pound baby potatoes, halved
2 tablespoons olive oil
2 cloves garlic, minced
1 teaspoon dried rosemary
1 teaspoon dried thyme
Salt and black pepper to taste
Chopped fresh parsley (for garnish)

Directions:
In a bowl, toss the halved baby potatoes with olive oil, minced garlic, dried rosemary, dried thyme, salt, and black pepper.
Preheat your air fryer to 375°F (190°C).
Place the seasoned potatoes in the air fryer basket.
Air fry for 18-20 mins, shaking the basket occasionally, until the potatoes are crispy on the outside and tender on the inside.
Garnish with chopped fresh parsley before serving.
Nutritional Values (per serving): Calories: 150 kcal Protein: 2g Carbohydrates: 21g Fat: 7g Fiber: 3g

Zucchini Parmesan Chips

Prep Time: 15 mins   Cooking Time: 10 mins
Servings: 4
Ingredients:
2 large zucchinis, sliced into rounds
1/2 cup breadcrumbs
1/4 cup grated Parmesan cheese
1/2 teaspoon garlic powder
1/2 teaspoon dried basil
1/2 teaspoon dried oregano
1/4 teaspoon paprika
Salt and black pepper to taste
Cooking spray

Directions:
In a bowl, combine breadcrumbs, grated Parmesan cheese, garlic powder, dried basil, dried oregano, paprika, salt, and black pepper.
Preheat your air fryer to 375°F (190°C).
Lightly coat the zucchini slices with cooking spray.
Dip each zucchini slice into the breadcrumb mixture, pressing the mixture onto both sides.

Place the coated zucchini slices in the air fryer basket, ensuring they are in a single layer.
Air fry for 8-10 mins until the zucchini chips are golden brown and crispy.
Serve hot as a healthy snack or side dish.
Nutritional Values (per serving): Calories: 122 kcal Protein: 5g Carbohydrates: 19g Fat: 2g Fiber: 2g

Parmesan Roasted Broccoli

Prep Time: 10 mins   Cooking Time: 10 mins
Servings: 4
Ingredients:
1 pound broccoli florets
2 tablespoons olive oil
1/4 cup grated Parmesan cheese
1/2 teaspoon garlic powder
Salt and black pepper to taste
Lemon wedges (for serving)

Directions:
Toss the broccoli florets with olive oil, grated Parmesan cheese, garlic powder, salt, and black pepper in a bowl.
Preheat your air fryer to 375°F (190°C).
Place the seasoned broccoli in the air fryer basket.
Air fry for 8-10 mins until the broccoli is tender and the edges are crispy.
Squeeze lemon juice over the roasted broccoli before serving.

Nutritional Values (per serving): Calories: 110 kcal Protein: 5g Carbohydrates: 9g Fat: 7g Fiber: 3g

Stuffed Turkey Peppers

Prep Time: 20 mins   Cooking Time: 18 mins
Servings: 4
Ingredients:
4 large bell peppers, tops removed, seeds, and membranes removed
1 pound ground beef turkey
1 cup cooked rice
1/2 cup diced tomatoes
1/2 cup diced onions
1/2 cup diced zucchini
1/2 cup shredded cheddar cheese
2 cloves garlic, minced
1 teaspoon Italian seasoning
Salt and black pepper to taste
Cooking spray

Directions:
In a skillet over medium heat, cook the ground beef or turkey until browned. Drain excess fat.
In a large bowl, combine the cooked meat, cooked rice, diced tomatoes, diced onions, diced zucchini, minced garlic, Italian seasoning, salt, and black pepper.
Preheat your air fryer to 375°F (190°C).
Lightly coat the outside of each bell pepper with cooking spray.
Fill each bell pepper with the meat and rice mixture.
Place the stuffed bell peppers in the air fryer basket.
Air fry for 16-18 mins until the peppers are tender and the filling is heated through.
Sprinkle shredded cheddar cheese on top of each pepper and air fry for an additional 2 mins until the cheese is melted and bubbly. Serve hot.
Nutritional Values (per serving): Calories: 352 kcal Protein: 25g Carbohydrates: 25g Fat: 16g Fiber: 4g

Crispy Eggplant Parmesan

Prep Time: 30 mins   Cooking Time: 15 mins
Servings: 4
Ingredients:
1 large eggplant, sliced into rounds
1 cup breadcrumbs
1/2 cup grated Parmesan cheese
2 eggs, beaten
1 cup marinara sauce
1 cup shredded mozzarella cheese
Salt and black pepper to taste
Cooking spray

Directions:
Dip each eggplant slice into the beaten eggs, allowing excess to drip off.
In a separate bowl, combine breadcrumbs, grated Parmesan cheese, salt, and black pepper.
Coat each eggplant slice with the breadcrumb mixture, pressing the mixture onto both sides.
Preheat your air fryer to 375°F (190°C).
Lightly coat the air fryer basket with cooking spray.
Place the coated eggplant slices in the air fryer basket, ensuring they are in a single layer.
Air fry for 8-10 mins until the eggplant is crispy and golden.
Top each eggplant slice with marinara sauce and shredded mozzarella cheese.
Air fry for an additional 2-3 mins until the cheese is melted and bubbly. Serve hot.
Nutritional Values (per serving): Calories: 281 kcal Protein: 14g Carbohydrates: 27g Fat: 13g Fiber: 5g

Garlic Butter Mushrooms

Prep Time: 10 mins   Cooking Time: 10 mins
Servings: 4
Ingredients:
1 pound button mushrooms, cleaned and halved
2 tablespoons melted butter
3 cloves garlic, minced
1 tablespoon fresh parsley, chopped
Salt and black pepper to taste
Lemon wedges (for serving)

Directions:
In a bowl, toss the halved mushrooms with melted butter, minced garlic, salt, and black pepper.
Preheat your air fryer to 375°F (190°C).
Place the seasoned mushrooms in the air fryer basket.
Air fry for 8-10 mins until the mushrooms are tender and slightly crispy.
Sprinkle with fresh chopped parsley and serve with lemon wedges for extra flavor.
Nutritional Values (per serving): Calories: 94 kcal Protein: 3g Carbohydrates: 6g Fat: 7g Fiber: 2g

Butternut Squash Fries

Prep Time: 15 mins   Cooking Time: 18 mins
Servings: 4
Ingredients:
1 butternut squash, peeled, seeded, and cut into fries
2 tablespoons olive oil
1/2 teaspoon paprika
1/2 teaspoon cinnamon
Salt and black pepper to taste
Maple syrup (for drizzling, optional)

Directions:
In a bowl, toss the butternut squash fries with olive oil, paprika, cinnamon, salt, and black pepper.
Preheat your air fryer to 375°F (190°C).
Place the seasoned butternut squash fries in the air fryer basket.
Air fry for 16-18 mins, shaking the basket occasionally, until the fries are crispy and golden.
Optionally, drizzle with maple syrup for a touch of sweetness before serving.
Nutritional Values (without maple syrup): Calories: 111 kcal Protein: 1g Carbohydrates: 18g Fat: 5g Fiber: 3g

Air Fryer Ratatouille

Prep Time: 20 mins   Cooking Time: 20 mins
Servings: 4
Ingredients:
1 small eggplant, diced
2 small zucchinis, diced
1 bell pepper, diced
1 onion, diced
2 cloves garlic, minced
1 can (14 ounces) diced tomatoes
1 tablespoon olive oil
1 teaspoon dried thyme
1 teaspoon dried basil
Salt and black pepper to taste
Fresh basil leaves (for garnish)

Directions:
In a large bowl, combine diced eggplant, diced zucchinis, diced bell pepper, diced onion, minced garlic, canned diced tomatoes (with juices), olive oil, dried thyme, dried basil, salt, and black pepper.
Preheat your air fryer to 375°F (190°C).
Place the vegetable mixture in the air fryer basket.

Air fry for 18-20 mins, tossing the mixture occasionally, until the vegetables are tender and slightly caramelized.
Garnish with fresh basil leaves before serving.
Nutritional Values (per serving): Calories: 92 kcal Protein: 2g Carbohydrates: 15g Fat: 4g Fiber: 5g

Corn on the Cob

Prep Time: 5 mins   Cooking Time: 12 mins
Servings: 4
Ingredients:
4 ears of corn, husked and cleaned
2 tablespoons melted butter
Salt and black pepper to taste

Directions:
Brush each ear of corn with melted butter and season with salt and black pepper.
Preheat your air fryer to 375°F (190°C).
Place the corn on the cob in the air fryer basket.
Air fry for 10-12 mins, turning the corn occasionally, until it's tender and slightly charred.
Serve hot, optionally with more melted butter for drizzling.
Nutritional Values (per serving): Calories: 108 kcal Protein: 2g Carbohydrates: 15g Fat: 5g Fiber: 2g

Garlic Roasted Green Beans

Prep Time: 10 mins   Cooking Time: 10 mins
Servings: 4
Ingredients:
1 pound fresh green beans, trimmed
2 tablespoons olive oil
2 cloves garlic, minced
1/4 teaspoon red pepper flakes (optional for a bit of heat)
Salt and black pepper to taste
Grated Parmesan cheese (for topping, optional)

Directions:
In a bowl, toss the trimmed green beans with olive oil, minced garlic, red pepper flakes (if using), salt, and black pepper.
Preheat your air fryer to 375°F (190°C).
Place the seasoned green beans in the air fryer basket.
Air fry for 8-10 mins, shaking the basket occasionally, until the green beans are tender and slightly crispy.
Optionally, sprinkle with grated Parmesan cheese before serving.
Nutritional Values (without Parmesan): Calories: 79 kcal Protein: 1g Carbohydrates: 6g Fat: 5g Fiber: 2g

Sweet and Spicy Carrot Fries

Prep Time: 15 mins   Cooking Time: 15 mins
Servings: 4
Ingredients:
4 large carrots, cut into thin fries
2 tablespoons honey
1 teaspoon Sriracha sauce (adjust for spiciness)
1/2 teaspoon ground cumin
Salt and black pepper to taste
Chopped fresh cilantro (for garnish)

Directions:
In a bowl, mix together honey, Sriracha sauce, ground cumin, salt, and black pepper.
Toss the carrot fries with the honey mixture until evenly coated.
Preheat your air fryer to 375°F (190°C).
Place the coated carrot fries in the air fryer basket.

Air fry for 12-15 mins, shaking the basket occasionally, until the carrot fries are tender and caramelized.
Garnish with chopped fresh cilantro before serving.
Nutritional Values (per serving): Calories: 93 kcal Protein: 1g Carbohydrates: 22g Fat: 0g Fiber: 3g

Lemon Herb Roasted Potatoes

Prep Time: 15 mins   Cooking Time: 20 mins
Servings: 4
Ingredients:
1 pound baby potatoes, halved
2 tablespoons olive oil
Zest and juice of 1 lemon
1 tablespoon fresh rosemary, chopped
1 tablespoon fresh thyme leaves
Salt and black pepper to taste
Fresh parsley (for garnish)

Directions:
In a bowl, toss the halved baby potatoes with olive oil, lemon zest, lemon juice, chopped fresh rosemary, chopped fresh thyme, salt, and black pepper.
Preheat your air fryer to 375°F (190°C).
Place the seasoned baby potatoes in the air fryer basket.
Air fry for 18-20 mins, shaking the basket occasionally, until the potatoes are crispy on the outside and tender on the inside.
Garnish with fresh parsley before serving.
Nutritional Values (per serving): Calories: 131 kcal Protein: 2g Carbohydrates: 20g Fat: 6g Fiber: 3g

Stuffed Mushrooms with Spinach and Cheese

Prep Time: 15 mins   Cooking Time: 10 mins
Servings: 4
Ingredients:
12 large white mushrooms, cleaned and stems removed
1 cup fresh spinach, chopped
1/2 cup cream cheese
1/4 cup grated Parmesan cheese
2 cloves garlic, minced
Salt and black pepper to taste
Fresh parsley (for garnish)

Directions:
In a bowl, combine chopped spinach, cream cheese, grated Parmesan cheese, minced garlic, salt, and black pepper.
Stuff each mushroom cap with the spinach and cheese mixture.
Preheat your air fryer to 375°F (190°C).
Place the stuffed mushrooms in the air fryer basket.
Air fry for 8-10 mins until the mushrooms are tender and the filling is heated through.
Garnish with fresh parsley before serving.
Nutritional Values (per serving): Calories: 115 kcal Protein: 5g Carbohydrates: 5g Fat: 8g Fiber: 1g

Cajun Sweet Potato Wedges

Prep Time: 15 mins   Cooking Time: 15 mins
Servings: 4
Ingredients:
2 large sweet potatoes, cut into wedges
2 tablespoons olive oil
1 teaspoon Cajun seasoning
1/2 teaspoon paprika
Salt and black pepper to taste
Sour cream or Greek yogurt (for dipping)

Directions:
In a bowl, toss the sweet potato wedges with olive oil, Cajun seasoning, paprika, salt, and black pepper.
Preheat your air fryer to 375°F (190°C).
Place the seasoned sweet potato wedges in the air fryer basket.

Air fry for 12-15 mins, shaking the basket occasionally, until the wedges are crispy on the outside and tender on the inside.
Serve hot with a side of sour cream or Greek yogurt for dipping.
Nutritional Values (per serving): Calories: 136 kcal Protein: 2g Carbohydrates: 21g Fat: 5g Fiber: 3g

Caprese Stuffed Portobello Mushrooms

Prep Time: 15 mins   Cooking Time: 12 mins
Servings: 4
Ingredients:
4 large Portobello mushrooms, stems removed
1 cup cherry tomatoes, halved
1/2 cup fresh mozzarella cheese, diced
1/4 cup fresh basil leaves, torn
2 tablespoons balsamic glaze
2 tablespoons olive oil
Salt and black pepper to taste

Directions:
In a bowl, combine halved cherry tomatoes, diced fresh mozzarella cheese, torn fresh basil leaves, balsamic glaze, olive oil, salt, and black pepper.
Stuff each Portobello mushroom cap with the tomato and mozzarella mixture.
Preheat your air fryer to 375°F (190°C).
Place the stuffed Portobello mushrooms in the air fryer basket.
Air fry for 10-12 mins until the mushrooms are tender and the filling is heated through.
Serve hot, drizzled with additional balsamic glaze if desired.
Nutritional Values (per serving): Calories: 149 kcal Protein: 7g Carbohydrates: 8g Fat: 11g Fiber: 2g

Coconut-Crusted Sweet Potato Fries

Prep Time: 15 mins   Cooking Time: 15 mins
Servings: 4
Ingredients:
2 large sweet potatoes, cut into fries
1/2 cup shredded coconut
1/4 cup panko breadcrumbs
1/2 teaspoon curry powder
1/2 teaspoon garlic powder
Salt and black pepper to taste
Cooking spray
Sweet chili sauce (for dipping)

Directions:
In a bowl, combine shredded coconut, panko breadcrumbs, curry powder, garlic powder, salt, and black pepper.
Toss the sweet potato fries with the coconut mixture until evenly coated.
Preheat your air fryer to 375°F (190°C).
Lightly coat the air fryer basket with cooking spray.
Place the coated sweet potato fries in the air fryer basket.
Air fry for 12-15 mins, shaking the basket occasionally, until the fries are crispy and golden.
Serve hot with sweet chili sauce for dipping.
Nutritional Values (per serving, without sauce): Calories: 150 kcal Protein: 2g Carbohydrates: 24g Fat: 6g Fiber: 4g

Crispy Broccoli Tots

Prep Time: 20 mins   Cooking Time: 10 mins
Servings: 4
Ingredients:
2 cups broccoli florets, steamed and finely chopped
1/2 cup breadcrumbs
1/4 cup grated Parmesan cheese
1/4 cup shredded cheddar cheese
1/4 cup diced onions
1 egg, beaten
1/2 teaspoon garlic powder
Salt and black pepper to taste
Ketchup or ranch dressing (for dipping)

Directions:

In a bowl, combine finely chopped broccoli florets, breadcrumbs, grated Parmesan cheese, shredded cheddar cheese, diced onions, beaten egg, garlic powder, salt, and black pepper.
Form the mixture into tot-shaped pieces.
Preheat your air fryer to 375°F (190°C).
Lightly coat the air fryer basket with cooking spray.
Place the broccoli tots in the air fryer basket.
Air fry for 8-10 mins until the tots are crispy and golden.
Serve hot with ketchup or ranch dressing for dipping.
Nutritional Values (per serving, without sauce): Calories: 120 kcal Protein: 6g Carbohydrates: 11g Fat: 6g Fiber: 3g

Balsamic-Glazed Brussel Sprouts

Prep Time: 10 mins   Cooking Time: 15 mins
Servings: 4
Ingredients:
1 pound Brussels sprouts, trimmed and halved
2 tablespoons olive oil
2 tablespoons balsamic vinegar
1 tablespoon honey
Salt and black pepper to taste
Chopped pecans (for garnish)

Directions:
In a bowl, toss the halved Brussels sprouts with olive oil, balsamic vinegar, honey, salt, and black pepper.
Preheat your air fryer to 375°F (190°C).
Place the seasoned Brussels sprouts in the air fryer basket.
Air fry for 12-15 mins, shaking the basket occasionally, until the Brussels sprouts are tender and caramelized.
Garnish with chopped pecans before serving.
Nutritional Values (per serving): Calories: 110 kcal Protein: 3g Carbohydrates: 18g Fat: 4g Fiber: 4g

Asparagus with Lemon and Parmesan

Prep Time: 10 mins   Cooking Time: 8 mins
Servings: 4
Ingredients:
1 bunch asparagus spears, trimmed
2 tablespoons olive oil
Zest and juice of 1 lemon
1/4 cup grated Parmesan cheese
Salt and black pepper to taste

Directions:

Toss the trimmed asparagus spears with olive oil, lemon zest, lemon juice, grated Parmesan cheese, salt, and black pepper in a bowl.
Preheat your air fryer to 375°F (190°C).
Place the seasoned asparagus in the air fryer basket.
Air fry for 6-8 mins until the asparagus is tender and lightly browned.
Serve hot, drizzled with extra lemon juice if desired.
Nutritional Values (per serving): Calories: 97 kcal Protein: 4g Carbohydrates: 6g Fat: 7g Fiber: 2g

Crispy Onion Rings

Prep Time: 15 mins   Cooking Time: 8 mins
Servings: 4
Ingredients:
2 large onions, cut into rings
1 cup buttermilk
1 cup flour
1 teaspoon paprika
1/2 teaspoon garlic powder
Salt and black pepper to taste
Cooking spray

Directions:

Soak the onion rings in buttermilk for 10-15 mins.
In a bowl, mix flour, paprika, garlic powder, salt, and black pepper.
Remove the onion rings from the buttermilk and coat them in the flour mixture.
Preheat your air fryer to 375°F (190°C).
Lightly coat the air fryer basket with cooking spray.
Place the coated onion rings in the air fryer basket in a single layer.

Air fry for 6-8 mins until the onion rings are crispy and golden.
Serve hot with your favorite dipping sauce.
Nutritional Values (per serving): Calories: 181 kcal Protein: 3g Carbohydrates: 36g Fat: 1g Fiber: 2g

Teriyaki Glazed Green Beans

Prep Time: 10 mins   Cooking Time: 10 mins
Servings: 4
Ingredients:
1 pound fresh green beans, trimmed
1/4 cup teriyaki sauce
2 tablespoons soy sauce
2 tablespoons honey
1 teaspoon sesame seeds
1 teaspoon sesame oil
Salt and black pepper to taste

Directions:

In a bowl, mix teriyaki sauce, soy sauce, honey, sesame seeds, sesame oil, salt, and black pepper.
Toss the trimmed green beans with the teriyaki mixture until evenly coated.
Preheat your air fryer to 375°F (190°C).
Place the seasoned green beans in the air fryer basket.
Air fry for 8-10 mins until the green beans are tender and glazed. Serve hot.
Nutritional Values (per serving): Calories: 103 kcal Protein: 2g Carbohydrates: 19g Fat: 2g Fiber: 2g

Roasted Red Pepper Hummus

Prep Time: 10 mins   Cooking Time: 0 mins
Servings: 6
Ingredients:
1 can (15 ounces) chickpeas, drained and rinsed
2 roasted red peppers (from a jar), drained and chopped
2 tablespoons tahini
2 cloves garlic, minced
Juice of 1 lemon
2 tablespoons olive oil
1/2 teaspoon ground cumin
Salt and black pepper to taste
Pita bread or vegetable sticks (for dipping)

Directions:
In a food processor, combine chickpeas, roasted red peppers, tahini, minced garlic, lemon juice, olive oil, ground cumin, salt, and black pepper.
Blend until smooth and creamy.
Transfer the roasted red pepper hummus to a serving bowl.
Serve with pita bread or vegetable sticks for dipping.
Nutritional Values (without pita or veggies): Calories: 124 kcal Protein: 4g Carbohydrates: 11g Fat: 7g Fiber: 3g

Zucchini Chips

Prep Time: 15 mins   Cooking Time: 10 mins
Servings: 2
Ingredients:
1/2 teaspoon garlic powder
1/2 teaspoon dried oregano
Salt and black pepper to taste
2 medium zucchinis
1 cup panko breadcrumbs
1/2 cup grated Parmesan cheese
1/4 olive oil
Marinara sauce (for dipping)

Directions:
In a bowl, combine panko breadcrumbs, Parmesan cheese, garlic powder, oregano, salt, and black pepper.
Dip zucchini into the breadcrumb mixture, pressing the mixture onto both sides.
Preheat your air fryer to 375°F (190°C).

Lightly coat the air fryer basket with olive oil. Place the coated zucchini slices in the air fryer basket.
Air fry for 8-10 mins until the zucchini chips are crispy and golden.
Serve hot with marinara sauce for dipping.
Nutritional Values (per serving, without sauce): Calories: 102 kcal Protein: 5g Carbohydrates: 12g Fat: 2g Fiber: 2g

Garlic Parmesan Roasted Brussels Sprouts

Prep Time: 10 mins   Cooking Time: 15 mins
Servings: 4
Ingredients:
1 pound Brussels sprouts, trimmed and halved
2 tablespoons olive oil
1/4 cup grated Parmesan cheese
2 cloves garlic, minced
Salt and black pepper to taste

Directions:
Toss the trimmed Brussels sprouts with olive oil, grated Parmesan cheese, minced garlic, salt, and black pepper in a bowl.
Preheat your air fryer to 375°F (190°C).
Place the seasoned Brussels sprouts in the air fryer basket.
Air fry for 12-15 mins, shaking the basket occasionally, until the Brussels sprouts are tender and the cheese is golden and crispy.
Serve hot.
Nutritional Values (per serving): Calories: 120 kcal Protein: 5g Carbohydrates: 9g Fat: 8g Fiber: 4g

Stuffed Beef Peppers

Prep Time: 20 mins   Cooking Time: 15 mins
Servings: 4
Ingredients:
4 large bell peppers, any color
1 cup cooked quinoa
1 cup cooked ground beef
1 cup diced tomatoes
1/2 cup black beans, drained and rinsed
1/2 cup shredded cheddar cheese
1/2 teaspoon chili powder
Salt and black pepper to taste
Fresh cilantro (for garnish)

Directions:
Cut the tops off the bell peppers and remove the seeds and membranes.
In a bowl, combine cooked quinoa, cooked ground turkey or beef, diced tomatoes, black beans, shredded cheddar cheese, chili powder, salt, and black pepper.
Stuff each bell pepper with the quinoa and meat mixture.
Preheat your air fryer to 375°F (190°C).
Place the stuffed bell peppers in the air fryer basket.
Air fry for 12-15 mins until the peppers are tender and the filling is heated through.
Garnish with fresh cilantro before serving.
Nutritional Values (per serving): Calories: 300 kcal Protein: 20g Carbohydrates: 32g Fat: 10g Fiber: 7g

Cinnamon Sugar Sweet Potato Fries

Prep Time: 15 mins   Cooking Time: 12 mins
Servings: 4
Ingredients:
2 large sweet potatoes, cut into fries
2 tablespoons melted butter
2 tablespoons granulated sugar
1 teaspoon ground cinnamon
Pinch of salt

Directions:
Brush each sweet potato fry with melted butter.
In a separate bowl, combine granulated sugar, ground cinnamon, and a pinch of salt.

Toss the sweet potato fries in the cinnamon sugar mixture until evenly coated.
Preheat your air fryer to 375°F (190°C).
Place the coated sweet potato fries in the air fryer basket.
Air fry for 10-12 mins until the fries are crispy and caramelized. Serve hot.
Nutritional Values (per serving): Calories: 150 kcal Protein: 1g Carbohydrates: 30g Fat: 4g Fiber: 4g

Garlic Parmesan Zucchini Noodles

Prep Time: 10 mins   Cooking Time: 8 mins
Servings: 4
Ingredients:
4 medium zucchinis, spiralized into noodles
2 tablespoons olive oil
2 cloves garlic, minced
1/4 cup grated Parmesan cheese
Salt and black pepper to taste
Chopped fresh parsley (for garnish)

Directions:
In a large skillet, heat olive oil over medium-high heat. Add minced garlic and sauté for 1-2 mins until fragrant.
Add the zucchini noodles to the skillet and sauté for 3-4 mins until they start to soften.
Transfer the sautéed zucchini noodles to a bowl, sprinkle with grated Parmesan cheese, salt, and black pepper.
Preheat your air fryer to 375°F (190°C).
Place the seasoned zucchini noodles in the air fryer basket.
Air fry for 5-8 mins until the noodles are tender and lightly crispy.
Garnish with chopped fresh parsley before serving.
Nutritional Values (per serving): Calories: 111 kcal Protein: 3g Carbohydrates: 6g Fat: 7g Fiber: 2g

CHAPTER 9
LAMB RECIPES

Air Fryer Lamb Chops

Prep Time: 15 mins   Cooking Time: 10 mins
Servings: 2
Ingredients:
4 lamb chops
2 tablespoons olive oil
2 cloves garlic, minced
1 teaspoon dried rosemary
Salt and black pepper to taste
Fresh rosemary sprigs for garnish (optional)

Directions:
In a bowl, mix olive oil, minced garlic, dried rosemary, salt, and black pepper.
Coat each lamb chop with the garlic and rosemary mixture, ensuring they are evenly coated.
Preheat your air fryer to 400°F (200°C).
Place the lamb chops in the air fryer basket in a single layer.
Air fry for 8-10 mins for medium-rare, or adjust the time for your desired level of doneness.
Garnish with fresh rosemary sprigs if desired and serve hot.
Nutritional Values (per serving): Calories: 304 kcal Protein: 22g Carbohydrates: 1g Fat: 23g Fiber: 0g

Air Fryer Lamb Kebabs

Prep Time: 20 mins   Cooking Time: 12 mins
Servings: 4
Ingredients:
1 pound lamb cubes, boneless
1 red bell pepper, cut into chunks
1 red onion, cut into chunks
2 tablespoons olive oil
2 cloves garlic, minced
1 teaspoon ground cumin
1 teaspoon ground paprika
Salt and black pepper to taste
Wooden skewers, soaked in water
Lemon wedges and tzatziki sauce (for serving)

Directions:
In a bowl, combine olive oil, minced garlic, ground cumin, ground paprika, salt, and black pepper.

Thread the lamb cubes, red bell pepper chunks, and red onion chunks onto the soaked wooden skewers, alternating between them.
Brush the skewers with the olive oil and spice mixture.
Preheat your air fryer to 375°F (190°C).
Place the lamb kebabs in the air fryer basket.
Air fry for 10-12 mins, turning halfway through, until the lamb is cooked to your desired level of doneness and the vegetables are tender.
Serve hot with lemon wedges and tzatziki sauce for dipping.
Nutritional Values (per serving, without sauce): Calories: 282 kcal Protein: 18g Carbohydrates: 7g Fat: 19g Fiber: 2g

Air Fryer Lamb Meatballs

Prep Time: 20 mins   Cooking Time: 12 mins
Servings: 4
Ingredients:
1 pound ground lamb
1/2 cup breadcrumbs
1/4 cup finely chopped red onion
2 cloves garlic, minced
1 teaspoon ground cumin
1 teaspoon ground coriander
1/2 teaspoon paprika
Salt and black pepper to taste
Cooking spray
Tzatziki sauce (for dipping)

Directions:
In a bowl, combine ground lamb, breadcrumbs, finely chopped red onion, minced garlic, ground cumin, ground coriander, paprika, salt, and black pepper.
Shape the mixture into meatballs.
Preheat your air fryer to 375°F (190°C).
Lightly coat the air fryer basket with cooking spray.
Place the lamb meatballs in the air fryer basket in a single layer.
Air fry for 10-12 mins until the meatballs are browned and cooked through.
Serve hot with tzatziki sauce for dipping.
Nutritional Values (per serving, without sauce): Calories: 316 kcal Protein: 18g Carbohydrates: 9g Fat: 24g Fiber: 1g

Moroccan Lamb Skewers

Prep Time: 25 mins   Cooking Time: 12 mins
Servings: 4
Ingredients:
1 pound lamb cubes, boneless
1/2 cup plain Greek yogurt
2 tablespoons olive oil
2 teaspoons ground cumin
1 teaspoon ground coriander
1/2 teaspoon ground cinnamon
Salt and black pepper to taste
Wooden skewers, soaked in water
Fresh cilantro leaves (for garnish)

Directions:
In a bowl, combine plain Greek yogurt, olive oil, ground cumin, ground coriander, ground cinnamon, salt, and black pepper.
Thread the lamb cubes onto the soaked wooden skewers.
Coat the lamb skewers with the yogurt and spice mixture.
Preheat your air fryer to 375°F (190°C).
Place the lamb skewers in the air fryer basket.
Air fry for 10-12 mins, turning halfway through, until the lamb is cooked to your desired level of doneness.
Garnish with fresh cilantro leaves and serve hot.
Nutritional Values (without garnish): Calories: 294 kcal Protein: 20g Carbohydrates: 4g Fat: 21g Fiber: 1g

Lamb and Vegetable Stir-Fry

Prep Time: 20 mins   Cooking Time: 10 mins
Servings: 4
Ingredients:
1 pound lamb strips, boneless
2 cups mixed vegetables (bell peppers, broccoli, snow peas, carrots), sliced
2 tablespoons soy sauce
2 cloves garlic, minced
1 teaspoon ginger, minced
1 tablespoon sesame oil
Salt and black pepper to taste
Sesame seeds and green onions (for garnish)
Cooked rice (for serving)
Directions:
In a bowl, mix soy sauce, minced garlic, minced ginger, sesame oil, salt, and black pepper.

Place lamb strips and mixed vegetables in a large bowl and pour the soy sauce mixture over them. Toss to coat.
Preheat your air fryer to 400°F (200°C).
Place the lamb and vegetable mixture in the air fryer basket.
Air fry for 8-10 mins, stirring halfway through, until the lamb is cooked, and vegetables are tender.
Garnish with sesame seeds and chopped green onions.
Serve over cooked rice.
Nutritional Values (per serving, without rice): Calories: 329 kcal Protein: 24g Carbohydrates: 12g Fat: 20g Fiber: 4g

Air Fryer Lamb Gyros

Prep Time: 30 mins   Cooking Time: 12 mins
Servings: 4
Ingredients:
1 pound lamb shoulder, thinly sliced
1 red onion, thinly sliced
2 cloves garlic, minced
1 teaspoon dried oregano
Juice of 1 lemon
Salt and black pepper to taste
Pita bread
Tzatziki sauce, diced tomatoes, and shredded lettuce (for serving)

Directions:
In a bowl, mix thinly sliced lamb, minced garlic, dried oregano, lemon juice, salt, and black pepper. Let it marinate for 20-30 mins.
Preheat your air fryer to 400°F (200°C).
Place the marinated lamb slices in the air fryer basket in a single layer.
Air fry for 10-12 mins, turning once, until the lamb is browned and cooked through.
Warm the pita bread in the air fryer for a minute.
Assemble the gyros with lamb slices, thinly sliced red onion, diced tomatoes, shredded lettuce, and tzatziki sauce.
Serve hot.
Nutritional Values (without toppings): Calories: 306 kcal Protein: 18g Carbohydrates: 20g Fat: 15g Fiber: 2g

Air Fryer Moroccan Lamb Chops

Prep Time: 30 mins   Cooking Time: 12 mins
Servings: 4
Ingredients:
8 lamb chops
2 tablespoons olive oil
2 teaspoons ground cumin
1/2 teaspoon ground paprika
Salt and black pepper to taste
1 teaspoon ground coriander
1 teaspoon ground cinnamon

Directions:
In a bowl, combine olive oil, ground cumin, ground coriander, ground cinnamon, ground paprika, salt, and black pepper.
Coat each lamb chop with the spice mixture, ensuring they are evenly coated.
Preheat your air fryer to 400°F (200°C).
Place the lamb chops in the air fryer basket in a single layer.
Air fry for 10-12 mins, turning halfway through, until the lamb chops are cooked to your desired level of doneness.
Serve hot.
Nutritional Values (without garnish): Calories: 287 kcal Protein: 26g Carbohydrates: 1g Fat: 20g Fiber: 0g

Air Fryer Lamb and Spinach Stuffed Peppers

Prep Time: 35 mins   Cooking Time: 15 mins
Servings: 4
Ingredients:
4 large bell peppers, halved and seeds removed
1 pound ground lamb
1 cup cooked rice
1/2 cup chopped spinach
1/4 cup diced tomatoes
2 cloves garlic, minced
1 teaspoon dried oregano
Salt and black pepper to taste
1/2 cup shredded mozzarella cheese
Fresh parsley leaves (for garnish)
Directions:
In a skillet, cook the ground lamb until browned. Drain any excess fat.

In a bowl, combine cooked lamb, cooked rice, chopped spinach, diced tomatoes, minced garlic, dried oregano, salt, and black pepper.
Preheat your air fryer to 375°F (190°C).
Stuff each bell pepper half with the lamb and rice mixture.
Place the stuffed peppers in the air fryer basket.
Air fry for 12-15 mins until the peppers are tender and the filling is heated through.
Sprinkle shredded mozzarella cheese on top and air fry for an additional 2 mins until the cheese is melted and bubbly.
Garnish with fresh parsley leaves and serve hot.
Nutritional Values (without garnish): Calories: 382 kcal Protein: 22g Carbohydrates: 23g Fat: 23g Fiber: 3g

Air Fryer Lamb Samosas

Prep Time: 30 mins   Cooking Time: 12 mins
Servings: 4
Ingredients:
1/2 pound ground lamb
1/2 cup frozen peas
1/4 cup finely chopped onions
2 cloves garlic, minced
1 teaspoon curry powder
Salt and black pepper to taste
8 sheets phyllo pastry, thawed
Cooking spray
Mint chutney (for dipping)
Directions:
In a skillet, cook ground lamb until browned. Drain any excess fat.
Add minced garlic, finely chopped onions, curry powder, salt, and black pepper to the cooked lamb.
Cook for a few mins until the onions are softened.
Stir in frozen peas and cook for another 2-3 mins.
Preheat your air fryer to 375°F (190°C).
Lay out one sheet of phyllo pastry and cut it into 3 equal strips.
Place a spoonful of the lamb mixture at the end of each phyllo strip, then fold into triangles, like folding a flag. Repeat with the remaining strips.
Lightly coat the samosas with cooking spray.
Place the samosas in the air fryer basket.
Air fry for 10-12 mins until they are crispy and golden.
Serve hot with mint chutney for dipping.
Nutritional Values (without chutney): Calories: 267 kcal Protein: 12g Carbohydrates: 22g Fat: 16g Fiber: 2g

Lamb Shawarma Wraps

Prep Time: 30 mins   Cooking Time: 10 mins
Servings: 4
Ingredients:
1 pound boneless lamb slices
2 tablespoons olive oil
2 cloves garlic, minced
1 teaspoon ground cumin
1 teaspoon ground coriander
1/2 teaspoon paprika
Salt and black pepper to taste
4 whole-wheat flatbreads or pita
Tzatziki sauce, sliced cucumbers, and tomatoes (for filling)
Directions:
In a bowl, mix olive oil, minced garlic, ground cumin, ground coriander, paprika, salt, and black pepper.
Coat the lamb slices with the spice mixture, ensuring they are evenly coated.
Preheat your air fryer to 375°F (190°C).
Place the lamb slices in the air fryer basket.
Air fry for 8-10 mins until the lamb is cooked to your desired level of doneness.
Warm the whole-wheat flatbreads or pita in the air fryer for a minute.
Assemble the wraps with cooked lamb slices, tzatziki sauce, sliced cucumbers, and tomatoes.
Roll them up and serve hot.
Nutritional Values (without filling): Calories: 300 kcal Protein: 18g Carbohydrates: 25g Fat: 15g Fiber: 4g

Air Fryer Lamb Curry

Prep Time: 30 mins   Cooking Time: 15 mins
Servings: 4
Ingredients:
1 pound lamb cubes
1 onion, chopped
2 cloves garlic, minced
1-inch piece of ginger, grated
2 tablespoons curry powder
1 cup coconut milk
Salt and black pepper to taste
Chopped fresh cilantro (for garnish)
Cooked rice (for serving)
Directions:
In a skillet, cook lamb cubes until browned. Drain any excess fat.

Add chopped onion, minced garlic, grated ginger, and curry powder to the cooked lamb. Cook for a few mins until the onions are softened.
Stir in coconut milk, salt, and black pepper. Simmer for 5-7 mins.
Preheat your air fryer to 375°F (190°C).
Place the lamb curry in an oven-safe dish and put it in the air fryer.
Air fry for 10-12 mins until the curry is heated through.
Garnish with chopped fresh cilantro and serve hot over cooked rice.
Nutritional Values (without rice): Calories: 354 kcal Protein: 20g Carbohydrates: 22g Fat: 14g Fiber: 3g

Air Fryer Lamb Burgers

Prep Time: 25 mins   Cooking Time: 10 mins
Servings: 4
Ingredients:
1 pound ground lamb
1/4 cup finely chopped red onion
1 clove garlic, minced
1 teaspoon ground cumin
1 teaspoon ground coriander
Salt and black pepper to taste
4 whole-wheat burger buns
Lettuce, tomato slices, and your favorite condiments (for serving)
Directions:
In a bowl, combine ground lamb, finely chopped red onion, minced garlic, ground cumin, ground coriander, salt, and black pepper.
Shape the mixture into 4 burger patties.
Preheat your air fryer to 375°F (190°C).
Place the lamb burger patties in the air fryer basket.
Air fry for 8-10 mins, turning once, until the burgers are cooked to your desired level of doneness.
Toast the whole-wheat burger buns in the air fryer for a minute.
Assemble the burgers with lettuce, tomato slices, and your favorite condiments.
Serve hot.
Nutritional Values (without condiments): Calories: 363 kcal Protein: 20g Carbohydrates: 26g Fat: 19g Fiber: 4g

Lamb and Vegetable Skewers with Chimichurri Sauce

Prep Time: 30 mins   Cooking Time: 12 mins
Servings: 4
Ingredients:
1 pound lamb cubes, boneless
1 red bell pepper, cut into chunks
1 yellow bell pepper, cut into chunks
1 red onion, cut into chunks
2 tablespoons olive oil
2 cloves garlic, minced
1/4 cup fresh parsley, chopped
1/4 cup fresh cilantro, chopped
1/4 cup red wine vinegar
Salt and black pepper to taste
Wooden skewers, soaked in water
Directions:
In a bowl, mix olive oil, minced garlic, chopped fresh parsley, chopped fresh cilantro, red wine vinegar, salt, and black pepper.
Thread the lamb cubes, red bell pepper chunks, yellow bell pepper chunks, and red onion chunks onto the soaked wooden skewers, alternating between them.
Brush the chimichurri sauce over the skewers.
Preheat your air fryer to 375°F (190°C).
Place the skewers in the air fryer basket.
Air fry for 10-12 mins, turning halfway through, until the lamb is cooked to your desired level of doneness and the vegetables are tender.
Serve hot with extra chimichurri sauce on the side.
Nutritional Values (without extra sauce): Calories: 292 kcal Protein: 18g Carbohydrates: 14g Fat: 17g Fiber: 3g

Air Fryer Lamb and Spinach Stuffed Mushrooms

Prep Time: 25 mins   Cooking Time: 10 mins
Servings: 4
Ingredients:
12 large white mushrooms, stems removed
1/2 pound ground lamb
1/2 cup chopped spinach
1/4 cup diced tomatoes
2 cloves garlic, minced
2 tablespoons grated Parmesan cheese
Salt and black pepper to taste
Cooking spray

Directions:
In a skillet, cook ground lamb until browned. Drain any excess fat.
Add chopped spinach, diced tomatoes, minced garlic, grated Parmesan cheese, salt, and black pepper to the cooked lamb. Cook for a few mins until the spinach wilts.
Preheat your air fryer to 375°F (190°C).
Lightly coat the air fryer basket with cooking spray. Stuff each mushroom cap with the lamb and spinach mixture.
Place the stuffed mushrooms in the air fryer basket. Air fry for 8-10 mins until the mushrooms are tender and the filling is heated through.
Serve hot.
Nutritional Values (per serving): Calories: 213 kcal Protein: 12g Carbohydrates: 7g Fat: 15g Fiber: 2g

CHAPTER 10
SNACKS AND APPETIZER RECIPES

Buffalo Cauliflower Bites

Prep Time: 15 mins   Cooking Time: 15 mins
Servings: 4
Ingredients:
1 head cauliflower, cut into florets
1/2 cup all-purpose flour
1/2 cup water
1 teaspoon garlic powder
1 teaspoon onion powder
1/2 cup buffalo sauce
2 tablespoons melted butter
Salt and black pepper to taste
Ranch or blue cheese dressing (for dipping)
Directions:
In a bowl, whisk together the flour, water, garlic powder, onion powder, salt, and black pepper to create a batter.
Dip each cauliflower floret into the batter, letting the excess drip off.
Preheat your air fryer to 375°F (190°C).
Place the battered cauliflower florets in the air fryer basket.
Air fry for 12-15 mins until the cauliflower is crispy and golden.
In a separate bowl, mix buffalo sauce and melted butter.
Toss the air-fried cauliflower in the buffalo sauce mixture until coated.
Serve hot with ranch or blue cheese dressing for dipping.
Nutritional Values (without dressing): Calories: 152 kcal Protein: 3g Carbohydrates: 15g Fat: 9g Fiber: 3g

Air Fryer Mozzarella Sticks

Prep Time: 15 mins   Cooking Time: 8 mins
Servings: 4
Ingredients:
12 mozzarella cheese sticks, cut in half
1 cup breadcrumbs
1/2 cup grated Parmesan cheese
2 eggs, beaten
1 teaspoon Italian seasoning
Marinara sauce (for dipping)
Directions:

In a bowl, combine breadcrumbs and grated Parmesan cheese.
Dip each mozzarella stick half into the beaten eggs, then into the breadcrumb mixture, ensuring they're evenly coated.
Preheat your air fryer to 375°F (190°C).
Place the coated mozzarella sticks in the air fryer basket.
Air fry for 6-8 mins until the sticks are golden and the cheese is melted.
Serve hot with marinara sauce for dipping.
Nutritional Values (without sauce): Calories: 205 kcal Protein: 11g Carbohydrates: 15g Fat: 11g Fiber: 1g

Crispy Potato Skins

Prep Time: 20 mins   Cooking Time: 15 mins
Servings: 4
Ingredients:
4 large russet potatoes
2 tablespoons olive oil
1 cup shredded cheddar cheese
1/2 cup cooked bacon bits
Sour cream and chopped green onions (for topping)
Directions:
Scrub and wash the russet potatoes. Prick them with a fork and microwave for 5-7 mins until slightly tender.
Cut the potatoes in half lengthwise and scoop out the flesh, leaving about 1/4 inch of potato on the skin.
Brush the potato skins with olive oil and place them in the air fryer basket.
Preheat your air fryer to 375°F (190°C).
Air fry the potato skins for 10-12 mins until they are crispy and golden.
Sprinkle shredded cheddar cheese and bacon bits on top.
Air fry for an additional 3-5 mins until the cheese is melted and bubbly.
Serve hot with sour cream and chopped green onions on top.
Nutritional Values (per serving): Calories: 288 kcal Protein: 11g Carbohydrates: 27g Fat: 15g Fiber: 2g

Air Fryer Spinach and Artichoke Stuffed Mushrooms

Prep Time: 20 mins   Cooking Time: 12 mins
Servings: 4
Ingredients:
12 large white mushrooms, cleaned and stems removed
1 cup frozen chopped spinach, thawed and drained
1/2 cup canned artichoke hearts, chopped
1/2 cup cream cheese
1/4 cup grated Parmesan cheese
2 cloves garlic, minced
Salt and black pepper to taste
Chopped fresh parsley (for garnish)

Directions:
In a bowl, combine chopped spinach, chopped artichoke hearts, cream cheese, grated Parmesan cheese, minced garlic, salt, and black pepper.
Stuff each mushroom cap with the spinach and artichoke mixture.
Preheat your air fryer to 375°F (190°C).
Place the stuffed mushrooms in the air fryer basket.
Air fry for 10-12 mins until the mushrooms are tender and the filling is heated through.
Garnish with chopped fresh parsley before serving.
Nutritional Values (per serving): Calories: 125 kcal Protein: 5g Carbohydrates: 6g Fat: 8g Fiber: 2g

Air Fryer Mini Empanadas

Prep Time: 30 mins   Cooking Time: 12 mins
Servings: 4
Ingredients:
1 package refrigerated pie dough
1 cup cooked ground beef or turkey
1/2 cup diced onions
1/2 cup diced bell peppers
1/2 cup diced tomatoes
1/2 cup shredded cheddar cheese
1 teaspoon chili powder
Salt and black pepper to taste
Sour cream or salsa (for dipping)

Directions:
Roll out the pie dough and cut it into small circles (use a glass or cookie cutter).

In a bowl, combine cooked ground beef or turkey, diced onions, diced bell peppers, diced tomatoes, shredded cheddar cheese, chili powder, salt, and black pepper.
Place a spoonful of the mixture onto each pie dough circle.
Fold the dough over to create a half-moon shape, and use a fork to seal the edges.
Preheat your air fryer to 375°F (190°C).
Place the mini empanadas in the air fryer basket.
Air fry for 10-12 mins until they are golden and crispy.
Serve hot with sour cream or salsa for dipping.
Nutritional Values (without dipping sauce): Calories: 233 kcal Protein: 9g Carbohydrates: 20g Fat: 13g Fiber: 2g

Crispy Avocado Fries

Prep Time: 15 mins   Cooking Time: 8 mins
Servings: 4
Ingredients:
2 ripe avocados, sliced into wedges
1 cup panko breadcrumbs
1/2 cup grated Parmesan cheese
2 eggs, beaten
1/2 teaspoon garlic powder
1/2 teaspoon paprika
Salt and black pepper to taste
Sriracha mayo or ranch dressing (for dipping)

Directions:
In a bowl, combine panko breadcrumbs, grated Parmesan cheese, garlic powder, paprika, salt, and black pepper.
Dip each avocado wedge into the beaten eggs, then into the breadcrumb mixture, ensuring they're evenly coated.
Preheat your air fryer to 375°F (190°C).
Place the coated avocado wedges in the air fryer basket.
Air fry for 6-8 mins until the avocado fries are crispy and golden.
Serve hot with sriracha mayo or ranch dressing for dipping.
Nutritional Values (without sauce): Calories: 228 kcal Protein: 6g Carbohydrates: 17g Fat: 15g Fiber: 6g

Air Fryer Crispy Chickpeas

Prep Time: 10 mins   Cooking Time: 15 mins
Servings: 4
Ingredients:
2 cans (15 ounces each) chickpeas, drained and rinsed
2 tablespoons olive oil
1 teaspoon paprika
1/2 teaspoon cumin
1/2 teaspoon garlic powder
Salt and cayenne pepper to taste (for added spice)

Directions:
Pat the chickpeas dry with a paper towel.
In a bowl, toss chickpeas with olive oil, paprika, cumin, garlic powder, salt, and cayenne pepper (if desired).
Preheat your air fryer to 375°F (190°C).
Place the seasoned chickpeas in the air fryer basket.
Air fry for 12-15 mins until the chickpeas are crispy and golden.
Let them cool before serving.
Nutritional Values (per serving): Calories: 148 kcal Protein: 6g Carbohydrates: 19g Fat: 6g Fiber: 6g

Portobello Mushrooms
Prep Time: 20 mins   Cooking Time: 10 mins
Servings: 4
Ingredients:
4 large portobello mushrooms, cleaned and stems removed
1/4 tablespoons salt
1/8 black pepper
3 tablespoons extra-virgin olive oil
1/4 teaspoon Italian seasoning

Directions:
Clean your portobello mushrooms thoroughly, then drizzle them with olive oil, salt and pepper.
Carefully put the mushrooms in the air fryer basket. Make sure you do not overlap them.

Air fry for 9-12 mins (both sides) until the mushrooms are tender and browned.
Serve hot.
Nutritional Values (per serving): Calories: 167 kcal Protein: 7g Carbohydrates: 9g Fat: 12g Fiber: 2g

Air Fryer Jalapeño Poppers

Prep Time: 20 mins   Cooking Time: 8 mins
Servings: 4
Ingredients:
8 large jalapeño peppers, halved and seeded
4 ounces cream cheese, softened
1/2 cup shredded cheddar cheese
1/2 cup cooked and crumbled bacon
1/2 teaspoon garlic powder
Salt and black pepper to taste
Toothpicks

Directions:
In a bowl, combine softened cream cheese, shredded cheddar cheese, cooked and crumbled bacon, garlic powder, salt, and black pepper.
Fill each jalapeño half with the cream cheese mixture.
Secure each popper with a toothpick to keep the filling intact.
Preheat your air fryer to 375°F (190°C).
Place the jalapeño poppers in the air fryer basket.
Air fry for 6-8 mins until the poppers are crispy and the cheese is melted.
Serve hot.
Nutritional Values (per serving): Calories: 163 kcal Protein: 7g Carbohydrates: 4g Fat: 13g Fiber: 1g

Stuffed Jalapeño Poppers with Sausage

Prep Time: 25 mins   Cooking Time: 10 mins
Servings: 4
Ingredients:
8 large jalapeño peppers, halved and seeded
8 ounces cream cheese, softened
1/2 cup cooked and crumbled sausage
1/2 cup shredded cheddar cheese
1/2 teaspoon garlic powder
Salt and black pepper to taste
Toothpicks

Directions:
In a bowl, combine softened cream cheese, cooked and crumbled sausage, shredded cheddar cheese, garlic powder, salt, and black pepper.
Fill each jalapeño half with the cream cheese and sausage mixture.
Secure each popper with a toothpick.
Preheat your air fryer to 375°F (190°C).
Place the stuffed jalapeño poppers in the air fryer basket.
Air fry for 8-10 mins until they are crispy and the filling is heated through.
Serve hot.
Nutritional Values (per serving): Calories: 239 kcal Protein: 8g Carbohydrates: 4g Fat: 19g Fiber: 1g

Air Fryer Sweet Potato Tots

Prep Time: 20 mins   Cooking Time: 10 mins
Servings: 4
Ingredients:
2 large sweet potatoes, peeled and grated
1/2 cup breadcrumbs
1/4 cup grated Parmesan cheese
1/2 teaspoon paprika
1/2 teaspoon garlic powder
Salt and black pepper to taste
Cooking spray
Ketchup or dipping sauce (for serving)

Directions:
In a bowl, combine grated sweet potatoes, breadcrumbs, grated Parmesan cheese, paprika, garlic powder, salt, and black pepper.
Shape the mixture into tots (small cylinders).
Preheat your air fryer to 375°F (190°C).

Lightly coat the air fryer basket with cooking spray.
Place the sweet potato tots in the air fryer basket in a single layer.
Air fry for 8-10 mins until the tots are crispy and golden.
Serve hot with ketchup or your favorite dipping sauce.
Nutritional Values (without sauce): Calories: 182 kcal Protein: 4g Carbohydrates: 31g Fat: 4g Fiber: 5g

Air Fryer Coconut Shrimp

Prep Time: 20 mins   Cooking Time: 10 mins
Servings: 4
Ingredients:
1 pound large shrimp
1/2 teaspoon garlic powder
1/2 teaspoon paprika
Salt and black pepper to taste
1 cup shredded coconut
1/2 cup panko breadcrumbs
2 eggs, beaten

Directions:
In a bowl, combine coconut, panko breadcrumbs, garlic powder, paprika, salt, and black pepper. Dip each shrimp into the beaten eggs, then into the coconut and breadcrumb mixture, pressing the mixture onto each shrimp to coat them evenly. Preheat your air fryer to 375°F (190°C).
Place the coated shrimp in the air fryer basket in a single layer.
Air fry for 8-10 mins until the shrimp are crispy and golden.

Nutritional Values (without sauce): Calories: 265kcal Protein: 16g Carbohydrates: 16g Fat: 18g Fiber: 1.5g

Stuffed Mushrooms with Crab

Prep Time: 25 mins   Cooking Time: 10 mins
Servings: 4
Ingredients:
12 large white mushrooms, cleaned and stems removed
8 ounces lump crab meat
1/2 cup cream cheese
1/4 cup grated Parmesan cheese
2 cloves garlic, minced
1/4 cup chopped fresh parsley
Salt and black pepper to taste

Directions:
In a bowl, combine lump crab meat, cream cheese, grated Parmesan cheese, minced garlic, chopped fresh parsley, salt, and black pepper.
Stuff each mushroom cap with the crab and cheese mixture.
Preheat your air fryer to 375°F (190°C).
Place the stuffed mushrooms in the air fryer basket.
Air fry for 8-10 mins until the mushrooms are tender and the filling is heated through.
Serve hot.
Nutritional Values (per serving): Calories: 213 kcal Protein: 14g Carbohydrates: 7g Fat: 15g Fiber: 2g

Air Fryer Mini Quesadillas

Prep Time: 20 mins   Cooking Time: 8 mins
Servings: 4
Ingredients:
8 small flour tortillas
1 cup shredded cheddar cheese
1/2 cup cooked and diced chicken or beef
1/4 cup diced bell peppers
1/4 cup diced onions
1/4 cup diced tomatoes
Cooking spray
Sour cream and salsa (for dipping)

Directions:
Place one tortilla on a flat surface and sprinkle with shredded cheddar cheese.
Add diced chicken or beef, diced bell peppers, diced onions, and diced tomatoes on top.
Place another tortilla on top to create a sandwich.
Repeat for the remaining tortillas.
Preheat your air fryer to 375°F (190°C).

Lightly coat the air fryer basket with cooking spray.
Place the mini quesadillas in the air fryer basket.
Air fry for 6-8 mins until they are crispy and the cheese is melted.
Serve hot with sour cream and salsa for dipping.
Nutritional Values (without dipping sauces): Calories: 296 kcal Protein: 15g Carbohydrates: 28g Fat: 14g Fiber: 2g

Air Fryer Onion Rings

Prep Time: 20 mins   Cooking Time: 8 mins
Servings: 4
Ingredients:
2 large sweet onions, cut into rings
1 cup all-purpose flour
2 eggs, beaten
1 cup panko breadcrumbs
1/2 teaspoon paprika
1/2 teaspoon garlic powder
Salt and black pepper to taste
Cooking spray
Ketchup or dipping sauce (for serving)

Directions:
Separate the onion slices into rings.
In a bowl, combine panko breadcrumbs, paprika, garlic powder, salt, and black pepper.
Dip each onion ring into the flour, then into the beaten eggs, and finally into the breadcrumb mixture, pressing the breadcrumbs onto the rings. Preheat your air fryer to 375°F (190°C).
Lightly coat the air fryer basket with cooking spray. Place the coated onion rings in the air fryer basket in a single layer.
Air fry for 6-8 mins until the onion rings are crispy and golden.
Serve hot with ketchup or your favorite dipping sauce.
Nutritional Values (without sauce): Calories: 184 kcal Protein: 6g Carbohydrates: 30g Fat: 4g Fiber: 2g

Air Fryer Bruschetta

Prep Time: 15 mins   Cooking Time: 5 mins
Servings: 4
Ingredients:
4 slices Italian bread, about 1/2 inch thick
2 large tomatoes, diced
1/4 cup fresh basil leaves, chopped
2 cloves garlic, minced
2 tablespoons balsamic vinegar
2 tablespoons olive oil
Salt and black pepper to taste
Fresh mozzarella cheese slices (optional)

Directions:
In a bowl, combine diced tomatoes, chopped fresh basil, minced garlic, balsamic vinegar, olive oil, salt, and black pepper.
Preheat your air fryer to 350°F (175°C).
Place the slices of Italian bread in the air fryer basket.
Air fry for 3-5 mins until the bread is toasted.
Top each toasted bread slice with the tomato mixture.
If desired, add a slice of fresh mozzarella cheese on top.
Air fry for an additional 2 mins until the cheese is slightly melted.
Serve hot.
Nutritional Values (without cheese): Calories: 141 kcal Protein: 3g Carbohydrates: 18g Fat: 6g Fiber: 2g

Teriyaki Chicken Wings

Prep Time: 25 mins   Cooking Time: 20 mins
Servings: 4
Ingredients:
2 pounds chicken wings
1/2 cup teriyaki sauce
2 tablespoons soy sauce
2 tablespoons honey
1/2 teaspoon garlic powder
1/2 teaspoon ginger powder
Chopped green onions (for garnish)

Directions:
In a bowl, mix soy sauce, honey, garlic powder, teriyaki sauce, and ginger powder to create the marinade.

Place chicken wings in a resealable plastic bag, pour in the marinade, and seal the bag. Refrigerate for at least 15 mins.
Preheat your air fryer to 375°F (190°C).
Remove the chicken wings from the marinade and place them in the air fryer basket.
Air fry for 18-20 mins, flipping halfway through, until the wings are crispy and cooked through.
Garnish with chopped green onions before serving.
Nutritional Values (per serving): Calories: 327 kcal Protein: 21g Carbohydrates: 14g Fat: 20g Fiber: 0g

Zucchini Fries

Prep Time: 20 mins   Cooking Time: 10 mins
Servings: 4
Ingredients:
2 large zucchinis, cut into fries
1 cup breadcrumbs
1/2 cup grated Parmesan cheese
1 teaspoon Italian seasoning
2 eggs, beaten
Salt and black pepper to taste
Marinara sauce (for dipping)

Directions:
Dip each zucchini fry into the beaten eggs, ensuring they're coated.
In a separate bowl, combine breadcrumbs, grated Parmesan cheese, Italian seasoning, salt, and black pepper.
Coat the egg-dipped zucchini fries with the breadcrumb mixture.
Preheat your air fryer to 375°F (190°C).
Place the coated zucchini fries in the air fryer basket.
Air fry for 8-10 mins until the fries are crispy and golden.
Serve hot with marinara sauce for dipping.
Nutritional Values (without sauce): Calories: 108 kcal Protein: 9g Carbohydrates: 20g Fat: 7g Fiber: 3g

Tandoori Chicken Skewers

Prep Time: 25 mins   Cooking Time: 12 mins
Servings: 4
Ingredients:
1 pound boneless, skinless chicken thighs, cut into chunks
1/2 cup plain Greek yogurt
2 tablespoons tandoori spice blend
Juice of 1 lemon
2 cloves garlic, minced
Salt and black pepper to taste
Wooden skewers, soaked in water

Directions:
In a bowl, combine Greek yogurt, tandoori spice blend, lemon juice, minced garlic, salt, and black pepper.
Add the chicken chunks to the marinade and coat them evenly. Refrigerate for at least 15 mins.
Thread the marinated chicken onto the soaked wooden skewers.
Preheat your air fryer to 375°F (190°C).
Place the chicken skewers in the air fryer basket.
Air fry for 10-12 mins until the chicken is cooked through and slightly charred.
Serve hot with your favorite dipping sauce or chutney.
Nutritional Values (per serving): Calories: 219 kcal Protein: 28g Carbohydrates: 4g Fat: 10g Fiber: 1g

Mini Calzones

Prep Time: 25 mins   Cooking Time: 12 mins
Servings: 4
Ingredients:
1 package refrigerated pizza dough
1/2 cup pizza sauce
1 cup shredded mozzarella cheese
1/4 cup sliced pepperoni
1/4 cup sliced black olives
1/4 cup diced green bell pepper
Cooking spray
Additional pizza sauce (for dipping)

Directions:
Roll out the pizza dough and cut it into smaller squares.

On each square, place a spoonful of pizza sauce, shredded mozzarella cheese, pepperoni slices, black olives, and diced green bell pepper.
Fold the dough over to create a mini calzone and seal the edges.
Preheat your air fryer to 375°F (190°C).
Lightly coat the air fryer basket with cooking spray.
Place the mini calzones in the air fryer basket.
Air fry for 10-12 mins until they are golden and crispy.
Serve hot with additional pizza sauce for dipping.
Nutritional Values (without extra sauce): Calories: 294 kcal Protein: 11g Carbohydrates: 28g Fat: 14g Fiber: 2g

Buffalo Butter Bites

Prep Time: 15 mins   Cooking Time: 15 mins
Servings: 4
Ingredients:
1 medium cauliflower head, cut into florets
1/2 cup buffalo wing sauce
1/4 cup melted butter
1 teaspoon garlic powder
1 teaspoon onion powder
Salt and black pepper to taste

Directions:
In a bowl, whisk together buffalo wing sauce, melted butter, garlic powder, onion powder, salt, and black pepper.
Toss the cauliflower florets in the buffalo sauce mixture until they are well coated.
Preheat your air fryer to 375°F (190°C).
Place the coated cauliflower florets in the air fryer basket.
Air fry for 12-15 mins until the cauliflower is tender and slightly crispy.
Serve hot.
Nutritional Values (without dressing): Calories: 124 kcal Protein: 3g Carbohydrates: 6g Fat: 10g Fiber: 2g

Garlic Parmesan Knots

Prep Time: 20 mins   Cooking Time: 8 mins
Servings: 4
Ingredients:

1 package refrigerated pizza dough

1/4 cup melted butter

2 cloves garlic, minced

2 tablespoons grated Parmesan cheese

1 tablespoon chopped fresh parsley

Salt and black pepper to taste

Directions:

Roll out the pizza dough and cut it into strips.

Tie each strip into a knot and place them on a plate.

In a bowl, combine melted butter, minced garlic, grated Parmesan cheese, chopped fresh parsley, salt, and black pepper.

Brush the garlic Parmesan mixture over each dough knot.

Preheat your air fryer to 375°F (190°C).

Place the garlic Parmesan knots in the air fryer basket.

Air fry for 6-8 mins until they are golden and cooked through.

Serve hot.

Nutritional Values (per serving): Calories: 241 kcal Protein: 3g Carbohydrates: 24g Fat: 15g Fiber: 1g

Air Fryer Falafel Bites

Prep Time: 30 mins   Cooking Time: 12 mins
Servings: 4
Ingredients:

1 can (15 ounces) chickpeas, drained and rinsed 1/4 cup diced onions

2 cloves garlic, minced

2 tablespoons fresh parsley, chopped

1 teaspoon ground cumin

1/2 teaspoon ground coriander

1/4 teaspoon cayenne pepper

Salt and black pepper to taste

2 tablespoons all-purpose flour

Cooking spray

Tahini sauce or yogurt sauce (for dipping)

Directions:

In a food processor, combine chickpeas, diced onions, minced garlic, fresh parsley, ground cumin, ground coriander, cayenne pepper, salt, and black pepper.

Pulse until well mixed but slightly chunky.

Transfer the mixture to a bowl and stir in all-purpose flour to bind the mixture.

Shape the mixture into small falafel balls. Preheat your air fryer to 375°F (190°C).

Lightly coat the air fryer basket with cooking spray. Place the falafel balls in the air fryer basket.

Air fry for 10-12 mins until the falafel is crispy and golden.

Serve hot with tahini sauce or yogurt sauce for dipping.

Nutritional Values (without sauce): Calories: 185 kcal Protein: 6g Carbohydrates: 28g Fat: 4g Fiber: 7g

Goat Cheese and Garlic Crostini

Prep time: 3 mins   Cooking time: 5 mins
Serves 4
Ingredients:
4 ounces (113 g) goat cheese
2 tablespoons minced fresh basil
1 whole wheat baguette
1/4 cup olive oil
2 minced garlic cloves

Directions
Heat up the air fryer to 380°F.
Slice the baguette into 1/2-inch-thick pieces.
Combine the olive oil and minced garlic in a small bowl, then use it to coat one side of each bread slice.
Arrange the garlic-infused bread slices in a single layer in the air fryer basket and air fry for 5 mins.
Meanwhile, in another small bowl, mix the goat cheese and finely chopped basil.
Take out the toasted bread from the air fryer, and generously spread a slender layer of the goat cheese mixture on each piece. Serve.
Nutritional Information (per serving): Calories: 248
Protein: 14g Fat: 18g Carbohydrates: 4g

Taco-Spiced Chickpeas

Prep time: 5 mins   Cooking time: 17 mins
Serves 3
Ingredients
1/2 teaspoon ground cumin
1/2 teaspoon salt
1/2 teaspoon granulated garlic
2 teaspoons lime juice
Oil (for spraying)
1 (15 1/2-ounce / 439-g) can of chickpeas, drained
1 teaspoon chili powder

Directions
Cover the air fryer basket with parchment paper and lightly apply oil spray. Put the drained chickpeas into the prepared basket.
Air fry at 390oF (199oC) for 17 mins, intermittently shaking or stirring the chickpeas and lightly spraying with oil every 5 to 7 mins.

In a small bowl, combine the chili powder, cumin, salt, and garlic.
When there are 2 to 3 mins left in the cooking time, sprinkle half of the seasoning mix over the chickpeas. Complete the cooking process.
Transfer the chickpeas to a medium-sized bowl, and toss them with the remaining seasoning mix and the lime juice. Serve promptly.
Nutritional Information (per serving): Calories: 412
Protein: 21g Fat: 13g Carbohydrates: 35g

Kale Chips with Sesame

Preparation time: 15 mins Cooking time: 8 mins
Serves 5
1/4 teaspoon garlic powder
1/2 teaspoon paprika
2 teaspoons sesame seeds
8 cups kale leaves, destemmed and torn into 2-inch pieces
1 1/2 tablespoons olive oil
3/4 teaspoon chili powder

Directions:
Heat up the air fryer to 350°F.
In a clean bowl, coat the kale with olive oil, chili powder, garlic powder, paprika, and sesame seeds, ensuring complete coating .
Place the seasoned kale into the air fryer basket and air fry for 8 mins, flipping the kale twice during the cooking process, until it turns crispy.
Serve while still warm.
Nutritional Information (per serving): Calories: 168
Protein: 7g Fat: 10g Carbohydrates: 7g

Roasted Grape Dip

Prep time: 10 mins   Cooking time: 8 to 12 mins
Serves 6
Ingredients
2 cups red seedless grapes, washed and dried
1 tablespoon apple cider vinegar
1 tablespoon honey
1 cup low-fat Greek yogurt
2 tablespoons 2% milk
2 tablespoons finely chopped fresh basil

Directions
Place the grapes in the air fryer basket and sprinkle them with cider vinegar and honey. Toss to ensure they are coated evenly. Air fry the grapes at 380°F (193°C) for 8 to 12 mins, or until they are soft. Carefully take them out of the air fryer.
In a medium-sized bowl, combine the yogurt and milk.
Gently fold in the roasted grapes and basil. Serve immediately, or refrigerate and chill for 1 to 2 hours before serving.

Nutritional Information (per serving): Calories: 320
Protein: 15g Fat: 14g Carbohydrates: 34g

Crispy Baked Mac and Cheese

Prep Time: 15 mins   Cooking Time: 12 mins
Servings: 4
Ingredients:
2 cups cooked macaroni
1 cup shredded cheddar cheese
1/2 cup shredded mozzarella cheese
1/2 cup milk
1/4 cup breadcrumbs
1/4 cup grated Parmesan cheese
Salt and pepper to taste

Directions:
In a bowl, mix cooked macaroni, cheddar cheese, mozzarella cheese, and milk.
Transfer the mixture to an air fryer-safe dish.
In a separate bowl, combine breadcrumbs, Parmesan cheese, salt, and pepper.
Sprinkle the breadcrumb mixture over the macaroni.

Air fry at 375°F (190°C) for 12 minutes or until golden and crispy.
Nutritional Information (per serving): Calories: 153
Protein: 8g Fat: 4g Carbohydrates: 23g

Air-Fried Chicken Pie

Prep Time: 20 mins   Cooking Time: 20 mins
Servings: 4
Ingredients:
2 cups cooked chicken, shredded
1 cup mixed vegetables (peas, carrots, corn)
1 cup chicken broth
2 tablespoons all-purpose flour
2 tablespoons butter
1 sheet puff pastry, thawed
Salt and pepper to taste

Directions:
In a saucepan, melt butter and stir in flour to create a roux.
Slowly add chicken broth, stirring until it thickens.
Mix in chicken and vegetables, season with salt and pepper.
Pour the mixture into an air fryer-safe dish.
Place the puff pastry sheet on top and cut a few slits for venting.
Air fry at 375°F (190°C) for 20 minutes or until the pastry is golden and the filling is bubbling.
Nutritional Information (per serving): Calories: 370
Protein: 20g Fat: 22g Carbohydrates: 24g

Low-Carb Lasagna

Prep Time: 25 mins   Cooking Time: 25 mins
Servings: 6
Ingredients:
1 pound lean ground beef
1 cup ricotta cheese
1 cup shredded mozzarella cheese
1/2 cup grated Parmesan cheese
1 egg
2 cups marinara sauce
Zucchini or eggplant slices (substitute for lasagna noodles)
Salt and pepper to taste

Directions:
Brown ground beef in a pan, season with salt and pepper.
In a bowl, mix ricotta cheese, mozzarella cheese, Parmesan cheese, and egg.
In an air fryer-safe dish, layer zucchini/eggplant, meat sauce, cheese mixture, and marinara sauce.
Repeat the layers.
Air fry at 375°F (190°C) for 25 minutes until bubbly and golden.
Nutritional Information (per serving): Calories: 340
Protein: 29g Fat: 19g Carbohydrates: 11g

Vegan Shepherd's Pie

Prep Time: 20 mins   Cooking Time: 18 mins
Servings: 4
Ingredients:
2 cups cooked lentils
1 cup mixed vegetables (carrots, peas, corn)
1 cup vegetable broth
2 cloves garlic, minced
1 onion, diced
2 tablespoons olive oil
Mashed potato topping

Directions:
In a pan, sauté onions and garlic in olive oil until translucent.
Add cooked lentils, mixed vegetables, and vegetable broth. Cook until heated through.
Transfer the mixture to an air fryer-safe dish.
Top with a layer of mashed potatoes.
Air fry at 375°F (190°C) for 18 minutes until the top is golden and the filling is hot.
Nutritional Information (per serving): Calories: 350
Protein: 15g Fat: 10g Carbohydrates: 52g

Veggie-Stuffed Calzones

Prep Time: 25 mins   Cooking Time: 15 mins
Servings: 4
Ingredients:
Pizza dough (store-bought or homemade)
1 cup marinara sauce
1 cup shredded mozzarella cheese
Assorted diced vegetables (bell peppers, mushrooms, spinach, etc.)
Olive oil for brushing

Directions:
Divide pizza dough into 4 portions and roll each into a circle.
On one half of each circle, layer marinara sauce, vegetables, and mozzarella cheese.
Fold the other half over to create a half-moon shape.
Seal the edges by pressing with a fork.
Brush the calzones with olive oil.
Air fry at 375°F (190°C) for 15 minutes or until golden brown.
Nutritional Information (per serving): Calories: 350
Protein: 12g Fat: 11g Carbohydrates: 53g

AIR FRYER
MEASUREMENT CONVERSION TABLE

Volume Equivalents (Liquid)

US STANDARD	METRIC (APPROXIMATE)	US STANDARD (OUNCES)
2 tablespoons	30 mL	1 fl. oz.
¼ cup	60 mL	2 fl. oz.
½ cup	120 mL	4 fl. oz.
1 cup	240 mL	8 fl. oz.
1½ cups	355 mL	12 fl. oz.
2 cups or 1 pint	475 mL	16 fl. oz.
4 cups or 1 quart	1 L	32 fl. oz.
1 gallon	4 L	128 fl. oz.

Air Fryer Temperatures

FAHRENHEIT (F)	CELSIUS (C) (APPROXIMATE)
250°	120°
300°	150°
325°	165°
350°	180°
375°	190°
400°	200°
425°	220°
450°	230°

Volume Equivalents (Dry)

US STANDARD	METRIC (APPROXIMATE)
⅛ teaspoon	0.5 mL
¼ teaspoon	1 mL
½ teaspoon	2 mL
¾ teaspoon	4 mL
1 teaspoon	5 mL
1 tablespoon	15 mL
¼ cup	59 mL
⅓ cup	79 mL
½ cup	118 mL
⅔ cup	156 mL
¾ cup	177 mL
1 cup	235 mL
2 cups or 1 pint	475 mL
3 cups	700 mL
4 cups or 1 quart	1 L

Weight Equivalent

US STANDARD	METRIC (APPROXIMATE)
½ ounce	15 g
1 ounce	30 g
2 ounces	60 g
4 ounces	115 g
8 ounces	225 g
12 ounces	340 g
16 ounces or 1 pound	455 g

CONCLUSION

We've reached the end of our air frying adventure, and what a delicious journey it's been! I hope you've enjoyed exploring the fantastic world of air frying as much as I have.

As we've seen, the air fryer isn't just an appliance; it's a culinary game-changer. It's the secret to achieving that perfect crunch without compromising your health, a tool for crafting healthier yet incredibly flavorful meals, and a kitchen companion that makes cooking a breeze.

Do not forget the importance of cleaning and maintaining your air fryer – a little care goes a long way in keeping it in mindblowing shape.

So, as you continue your culinary journey with your air fryer, remember that it's a tool of creativity and convenience. Use it to explore new flavors, enjoy tasty dishes, and make healthier choices.

Thanks for joining me on this tasty journey!!

INDEX OF RECIPES

Made in the USA
Middletown, DE
19 December 2023

46379286R00057